STIEGEL-TYPE ENAMELED DRUG BOTTLE

*Although similar bottles were made in Switzerland and Germany, a few characteristic designs
have been attributed to Stiegel*

AMERICAN
GLASS AND
GLASSMAKING

LURA WOODSIDE WATKINS

CRACKER BARREL PRESS
Southampton, N. Y.

CONTENTS

PLATES

~~~~~~

PLATES

∽∽∽∽∽∽∽∽∽∽∽∽∽∽∽∽∽∽∽∽∽∽∽∽∽∽∽

Chapter one

~~~~~~~~~~~~~~~~~~~~~~~~~~~~~~~~~~~~~

Glass and Its Manufacture

GLASSMAKING IS BOTH AN ART AND AN INDUSTRY, BOTH A CRAFT and a co-operative venture. While it demands on the part of the glass-blower a virtuosity comparable to that of a skilled musician, it also requires the brains and labor of many other persons to supplement his art and to carry on the various processes in a glasshouse. For this reason, it has never been easy to establish a glass manufacture.

Glass is one of the miracles of man's making. Compounded of the earthiest ingredients, it emerges from the fire as transparent as rock crystal. The best clear glass is composed of a silica, usually in the form of sand, a certain proportion of lead, potash, and carbonate of soda for alkalis, and small quantities of arsenic and manganese to offset the natural coloring agents. In early times calcined flints were utilized as silica in the making of clear glass: hence the term *flint* glass, which has ever since been applied to the lead metal originated by the English just before 1700.

Bottle and window glass contain no lead and appear in shades of aquamarine, green, olive, or amber. These colors result from impurities in the materials, which are not so carefully cleansed as are those used for lead glass. Much early bottle glass was so dark in color it was known as "black" glass, and, unless seen by transmitted light, it does indeed look black.

A clear glass made without lead—a soda-lime glass—was the rule in Continental glasshouses and in some manufactories in America. Such metal is lighter in weight than lead glass and does not respond with a bell-like ring when struck.

In early days the formulae for glass were governed by the quality of the materials and the irregular heat of the wood-burning furnaces. Decisions about ingredients rested with the *gaffer* or superintendent of the glasshouse until the time when chemists were especially employed for the purpose. The sand and other materials were kept in great bins in the mixing room, where they were shoveled together and thence carried on barrows to the furnaces. To every batch was added a certain proportion (about one-third) of old broken glass, or *cullet*, of the kind being made.

The furnace was the center of interest in a glasshouse. Small factories usually had but one. As an industry grew, it was not uncommon for it to have as many as five furnaces with their five chimneys. These circular structures, illustrated in Plate 1b, each accommodated from six to ten pots ranged around a central opening in the furnace floor above the fires on a lower level. Wood was the first fuel used, and great sections of forest were sacrificed for glassmaking. Early in the nineteenth century, even in New England, coal became available. Later on, the discovery of natural gas led to a revolution in the American glass industry. The adoption of a fuel so much cheaper and cleaner than coal resulted in the removal of most of the eastern glasshouses to Pennsylvania and Ohio, nearer the source of supply.

Men employed for the purpose made the glass pots, which were huge, thick containers built of clay from Stourbridge, England. They held from five hundred pounds to more than a ton of molten metal. As they soon cracked or were broken from the intense heat, generally lasting no longer than six weeks, they had to be frequently replaced. This process meant bringing the pots to white heat and setting them in position over a raging fire—one of the most arduous and dangerous duties in a glasshouse. Pots for bottle glass were open at the top, but flint-glass crucibles had to be covered in order to protect the metal from the smoke and gases of the fire. A small opening in the side was left for withdrawing the glass to be worked. After the pots were set, masonry was built up in front of them, leaving only the necessary openings.

The ingredients of a melt or batch were shoveled into the pots gradually until the whole was in a state of flux. Then the fires were increased. At this point the molten metal was too fluid to work, but, after a period of cooling, it was in a semi-solid condition and ready for the processes of

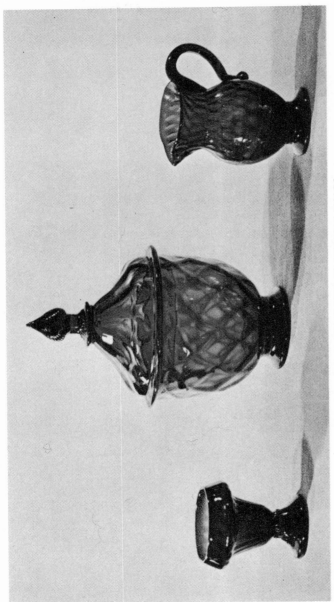

Plate II

STIEGEL-TYPE GLASS BLOWN IN PATTERN MOLDS

The expanded diamond design of the sugar bowl and creamer occurs frequently on glass made by Stiegel and his successors in Pennsylvania and Ohio

blowing or pressing. Glass has the quality of plasticity, so that it can be manipulated into any shape, and of great ductility, which makes it possible to draw it out evenly to great lengths.

The blowing of one small piece of glass requires the co-operation of several workmen. The master blower or gaffer of a *shop* does much of his work seated on a chair equipped with flat iron arms. He is first assisted by a *gatherer*, whose business it is to take up the needed quantity of sticky molten glass on the end of an iron blowpipe—a hollow rod enlarged at one end and about four or five feet long. This gathering he prepares in shape for blowing by rolling it back and forth on an iron table—the *marver*. He then hands it to the gaffer, who proceeds to inflate it, as in Plate 2, to elongate it by swinging the blowpipe about his head, or to compress it with tools to the approximate size and shape desired. At this point a *sticker-up* comes with a small glob of hot glass on the end of a solid iron rod known as a *pontil* or *punty* rod. This he affixes to the end of the glass bubble opposite the blowpipe, which the blower then breaks away from the glass with a sharp rap. The gaffer now works with the glass on the end of the punty rod, proceeding with the aid of a few simple wooden and iron tools to manipulate the glass into its finished form (Plate 3).

During the course of manipulation, the blowpipe or punty is laid across the arm of the blower's chair, with the bubble of glass at his right, and is rolled back and forth to insure symmetry, as in turning wood on a lathe. In this way, by means of a pronged tool (the *pucellas*), the glass-maker can compress the bubble from without or enlarge it from within by contracting or opening the arms of the instrument. With shears he can trim the lip, which can then be flared or fluted or otherwise shaped.

Meanwhile the white-hot glass has been cooling and must, if a complicated object is being made, be reheated again and again by presenting it to the flames at the *glory hole*. This was originally an opening in the large furnace, but was later a separate structure. Reheating restores the plasticity of the glass and softens its surface again to a smooth fire polish. Handles or stems and bases of goblets are additions to the first gather, which are brought by the blower's assistants and attached at the desired point, then cut off to the proper size with shears before the gaffer deftly shapes them with other tools. All these operations are executed very rapidly—in less time than it takes to describe them. The necessity for working with great speed and accuracy on the ever-cooling glass demands on the part of the glassblower a remarkable degree of virtuosity.

When the piece has attained its final form and has been received in a wooden tong held by a boy, the blower snaps it away from the punty rod and it is ready for cooling. The glass is still white hot. If cooled at room temperature, it would crack or fly to pieces. It therefore has to be left for a day or more in the long annealing oven, or *lehr* (leer), where it is moved on carriers through gradually diminishing temperatures until it can be taken into the open air at the other end. The rough scar left by the breaking away of the pontil rod is known as a *pontil mark*. In early days this was invariably left rough. After cutting was introduced, the pontil mark on better glass was ground off on the cutter's wheel, and only cheap or common wares were left with a scar.

Much glass is blown in molds. These are placed on the floor, or below the level of the floor, for the convenience of the blower with his long pipe. In molding, the gather is lowered into the mold and inflated until it has assumed the form or pattern. For certain objects the mold may be constructed in one part or, in order to avoid marring the pattern when the soft glass is withdrawn, it may be an open-and-shut device of two or more parts.

The pressing of glass as we know it today was an American invention developed in the 1820's. By this process glass is actually squeezed into shape in molds under pressure. At first this was effected by hand-operated machines; later, by screw presses that could apply more force to the plunger. The mold design, corresponding to the outside of the object, is usually, although not invariably, cut in the body of the mold, while the plunger, descending from above, bears the smooth shape of the interior of the finished piece of glass. Surrounding the plunger opening is a removable ring or rim that prevents any escape or overflow of the molten metal. In early practice, the required amount of glass was brought on a rod from the furnace and held over the mold, while an assistant sheared it away from the rod. Unless the gatherer had sufficient dexterity to flip the lump of glass over as it dropped from the shears, this cutting left a ridge or line that could be seen on the interior of the finished vessel. Such lines, known as *shear* or *scratch* marks, appear on a great deal of early pressed glass.

The business of pressing has been entirely mechanized in modern times, so that thousands of pieces can be turned out in a day. The famous Owens bottle machine has also taken over the labors of blowing for commercial containers.

It is agreed by those who are connoisseurs of the quality of glass that its best expression is effected by the manipulation of the material without extrinsic ornamentation. Its peculiar liquid character is thus caught, as it were, and arrested while still in motion. This may be seen in the shaping of lips and feet, the formation of handles, the application of threads or ribbons of glass, or in various forms of tooling, as exemplified, for instance, in the fashioning of Venetian glass. These types of plastic handling, where the glass itself is its own ornament, appear at their best in America in certain traditional forms, such as the lily-pad technique of South Jersey and in other offhand work from country glasshouses. In such glass the blowers played with the material and no further labor or expense was involved.

People of means, especially those who have newly acquired it, have always demanded elaboration. So it happened that, after America had reached a degree of prosperity, glass embellished with engraving, cutting, and enameling was produced. These processes are all outside of the actual making of the glass and are carried on as separate functions by artisans other than the blower.

Engraving is accomplished by holding the glass against a small revolving copper wheel or spindle, over which pours a stream of oil and emery powder. It requires great skill, as the liquid obscures the field, and the engraver works largely by feeling his way on designs that are also unseen, except in his imagination. Wheels of many different sizes, according to the requirements, are employed.

Cutting is a grinding process effected by the use of larger wheels fed with sand and water. The actual cutting of the pattern is followed by smoothing on a wheel of fine sandstone and by polishing on a wooden wheel supplied with emery and then with putty powder.

Etching is done, often in imitation of engraving, by the application of hydrofluoric acid to the intended design, the background being stopped out with a coating of wax or asphaltum to resist the action of the chemical. Entire objects are sometimes given a dull or mat finish by immersion in this acid.

Enameling is the process of painting on glass with colors that are themselves of a glassy substance. The work is completed by firing.

MIDWESTERN LACY DISH

Plate 1

a) THE BOSTON AND SANDWICH GLASS WORKS

Pendleton Brothers of Boston published this lithograph soon after the buildings were erected in 1825

b) BLOWING ROOM IN AN EARLY GLASSHOUSE

The activities of gathering, blowing, and shaping glass take place near the furnaces.
They are here shown in a woodcut from Ballou's Pictorial, January 20th, 1855

Plate 2

GLASSBLOWER AT WORK

*Seated in his glassmaker's chair, he is inflating a bubble, which has already
been partly shaped by the use of a wooden paddle*

Plate 3

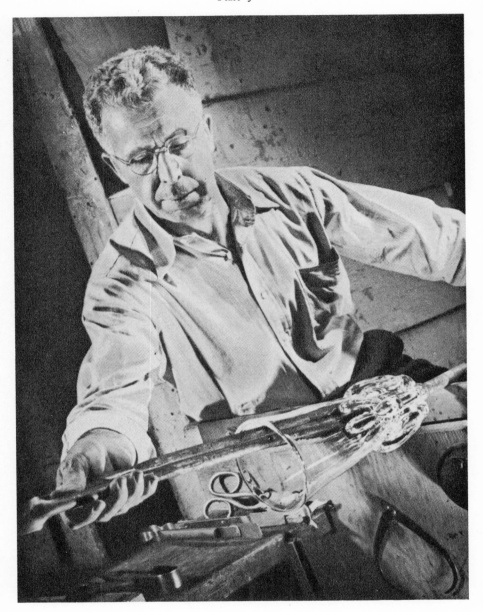

SHAPING A VASE

*Holding the glass by a punty rod attached to the base, the glassblower is
expanding it by pressure of the pucellas*

Plate 4

a) SEVENTEENTH-CENTURY BOTTLE

*This corresponds in shape to the earliest dated English
bottle and is no doubt similar to those made at Jamestown and Salem*

b) EIGHTEENTH-CENTURY BOTTLES OF DARK-GREEN GLASS

*From left to right: Case bottle made square to fit in a wooden chest. Chestnut bottle.
Wistarberg-type liquor bottle dated 1747. Snuff bottle*

~~~~~~

Chapter two

The Pioneer Glasshouses

GLASSMAKING WAS THE VERY FIRST INDUSTRY TO BE UNDERTAKEN in the Colonies. Strangely enough, although the need for window panes and containers in pioneer communities was acute, our first glass was not blown for local requirements, but for export. John Smith and his first little band of settlers at Jamestown, Virginia, observing the unlimited supply of fuel in the virgin forests and the sand to be had for the taking, conceived the idea of building a glasshouse to supply England and to lure immigrant workmen to this country. In 1608, with the second group of arrivals, came eight Dutch and Polish glassmen. It is known that the glasshouse was built about one mile north of the settlement and that samples of the product were shipped to London the following year. Although there was such abundance of materials, the workmen were not an industrious lot. When Captain Argall arrived as governor in 1617, the glasshouse was no longer running and the buildings had fallen into decay.

We can only conjecture what America's first glass may have been. As flint metal had not then been invented and articles of clear glass were so rare that few, even of the nobility, were familiar with them, it is probable that bottles of dark glass were the only output. They were doubtless similar to the seventeenth-century example in Plate 4a.

In spite of the failure of this first attempt, enough men in the London company were still willing to risk their capital for a second trial. Accordingly, in 1621, a Captain William Norton, whose "chief employment" was the making of beads, came over with six Italian glassblowers. He and his men were well lodged until they could select a site for the furnace that would be safe from surprise by the Indians. Since the Italian glass workers survived the massacre of 1622, it is evident that the second glasshouse was outside the village of Jamestown. This site has recently been discovered and partially excavated in a location about three-fourths of a mile from the original settlement. Although the trade beads so fre- quently found in Indian graves in the south-eastern United States have been attributed to these workmen, no evidence has as yet been unearthed to show that they made anything more than bottles and window panes.

A second pioneer venture in Salem, Massachusetts, left traces that remained as late as fifty years ago. In 1639, Ananias Concklin, Obadiah Holmes, and Lawrence Southwick, called "glass men" in records, were each granted two acres of land "adjoining to their houses" for the further- ance of a glasshouse project. They were joined in the following year by John Concklin, a practical glass worker, who was given five more acres abutting on the previous grants. This acreage was off the old Boston road (Aborn Street), on what is now Abbott Street in Peabody. In December 1641, the General Court of the province authorized the town of Salem to lend the proprietors thirty pounds, which they were to repay "if the work succeeded when they were able." No record of their activities in the ensuing years has as yet come to light. They are next heard of in 1645, when the Concklins petitioned the General Court for a settlement of their affairs with the "undertakers" (Holmes and Southwick). They said that the glass works had been neglected for three years and that they had not been paid. They petitioned for a release from their agreement so that they might seek work elsewhere.

For many years the site of this industry was called the "glasshouse field," and fragments of dark greenish glass used to be found near a stone wall that once bounded the property. While it seems certain that the Concklins actually blew glass, they probably achieved nothing more important than bottles.

During the Dutch occupation of New York, *i.e.* before 1664, Jan Smeedes ran a glass works on what is now South William Street, between Wall and Pearl Streets. Ten years later, Evert Duycking retired from the management of a glasshouse—possibly the same one—in favor of Jacob Melyer, whose descendants are said to have made glass in New York for several generations. The New York records are meager, but show at least that the Dutch were pursuing this industry in the seventeenth century.

William Penn, in a letter written in August 1683, mentions a Pennsylvania glass works. He speaks of a tannery, saw-mill, and glasshouse, "the last two conveniently posted for water carriage." A later record shows that the building stood in Shackmaxson, about one and a half miles north of Penn's town, in a section now within the city limits of Philadelphia. This, too, was probably a short-lived venture.

The pioneer attempts at glassmaking, then, took place in Jamestown (1608); Salem (1639); New York (before 1664); and Philadelphia (1683). Although nothing definite is known about the output of any of these concerns, we may safely conjecture that it was limited to window glass and to bottles similar to those in Plate 4. There is indication of some manufacture of the former at Philadelphia, where a "broad glass man," Joshua Tittery, from Newcastle-on-Tyne, was employed.

Until 1732 there is no further record of glassmaking in the Colonies. In that year there were two glasshouses in New York City. One of them, known as the "Glass-House Farm," appears on De Witt's *Farm Map of New York* on land facing the Hudson River near what is now 35th Street. Whether this was Melyer's glass works or the original location of a somewhat later establishment the scanty New York records do not show. Previous to 1752, Matthew Earnest, Samuel Bayard, Lodewyck Bamper, and Christian Hertell formed a partnership for the purpose of building a glasshouse. They made an agreement with one Johan Martin Greiner of Saxe-Weimar, Germany, to come to America to teach them the "Art & Mystery of Erecting & Building a Glass House & allso in Blowing & Making of Glass." He was to supervise every step in the construction of ovens and making of pots and he promised to remain in New York for a term of twenty years. The glass company agreed to pay Greiner twenty-four styvers for every one hundred quart bottles and three guilders for every fifty half-gallon flasks.

In November 1754, Thomas Lepper, storekeeper for the glasshouse, advertised bottles and "a Variety of other Glass Ware too tedious to mention." He also announced: "Gentlemen that wants Bottles of any size with their names on them, or any Chymical Glasses, or any other sort of Glass Ware, may by applying to said Lepper, have them with all Expedition." This New York company continued in operation until 1767. Although no specimens of its manufacture have been identified, it apparently produced some vessels other than mere bottles. It is possible that some Stiegel-type glass was made at the "Glass-House Farm."

The year 1739 marks the establishment of the first successful glass works in New Jersey. It was founded by Casper Wistar in Salem County, about two and a half miles from Allowaystown, and not far from Phila-delphia. Wistar was a German who had migrated to this country in 1717 at the age of twenty-one. He was the forerunner of hundreds of the same nationality who were responsible for the final success of American glass-making. Indeed, in the eighteenth century, the greater number of glassblowers were of Germanic origin, and it is to Germany that we must look for stylistic influences in much of our good early glass. At the time when Wistar built his glasshouse, he was a prominent business man in Philadelphia. Among other activities, he carried on the manufacture of brass buttons. He entered upon this new undertaking as a business venture and not because he had any knowledge of glassmaking. He therefore engaged four "glass experts," whose passage from Rotterdam he paid, and with whom he entered into an agreement whereby they were to teach him and his son the art of glassmaking, while he was to provide them with all the necessities for living and for building the glasshouse, together with one-third of the profits. Although these artisans came from Holland, their names indicate that they may have been German, not Dutch.

Casper Wistar died in 1752 and was succeeded by his son Richard in both of his manufactures. The Wistarberg works, as it was later known, ran continuously until the Revolution. In the Pennsylvania newspapers of 1769 Richard Wistar advertised window glass, common bottles of several types and sizes, case bottles, containers for snuff and mustard, besides chemical wares, such as retorts, globes, and tubes. Twenty-five years ago, when all South Jersey glass of whatever description was attrib-uted to the Wistarberg factory, it would have been a disappointment to learn that bottles were indeed its sole output. Nevertheless, the late Harry

Plate 5

a) STIEGEL-TYPE BOTTLE AND FLIP GLASSES

Characteristic motifs employed by Stiegel engravers are sunburst with bird, lily-of-the-valley, and the tulip

b) STIEGEL "DIAMOND DAISY" BOTTLE

This type of pattern-molded design occurs only on bottles of American origin and may almost certainly be attributed to Stiegel

c) STIEGEL-TYPE CLEAR-GLASS VASE

Paneling of the kind that appears on this vase was formed by blowing the gather into a part-sized mold with subsequent expansion

Plate 6

a) PRESENTATION POKAL

This piece was engraved at the Amelung works in Frederick, Maryland.
The inscriptions read: Old Bremen Success and the New Progress *and* New Bremen Glassmanufactory—1788 —North America, State of Maryland

b) AMELUNG FLIP GLASS

This was presented to the Boston Crown Glass Company of Boston, when their emissary visited the Amelung works. It is inscribed: Our best wishes for every Glassmanufactory in the United States. God bless the City of Boston. Made at the Glassmanufactory of New Bremen in Maryland the 23 Jan. 1789 by John Fr. Amelung & Company

Hall White, after examination of the Wistarberg site, stated that he found there only glass of the coarsest description. There is no question that many offhand pieces made by the blowers for presentation or for their own use must have been blown in this early works, but it is now impossible to distinguish them from the many similar glasses that emanated from later New Jersey factories. The lily-pad technique, which was long considered peculiar to Wistarberg, undoubtedly originated there, but it was also practised extensively in the later glasshouses that were an outgrowth of this early establishment. The South Jersey area has long been a hunting ground for fine primitive specimens: some of them could have been made by Wistar's "glass experts."

The common spirit bottle of the mid-eighteenth century was formed like a shortened cylinder, with medium-long neck, and with base pushed up to give a deceptive appearance as to its capacity. Case bottles were blown in molds to give them square corners so that they could be packed into the compartments of a wooden chest. Snuff bottles were also molded to a squarish form. These familiar types, shown in Plate 4b, were the kind that comprised Wistar's commercial output.

An early glass industry was carried on for a time in Quincy, Massachusetts. Founded by a group of Boston business men, it was part of a scheme to establish various manufactures that were to be manned by a colony of Germans brought to America for the purpose. The village created in 1752 has ever since been known as Germantown. Joseph Palmer was the agent or manager of the glasshouse. In a manuscript letter owned by the Massachusetts Historical Society, he explains that the purpose of the project was to make bottles for shipping New England cider to the West Indies in exchange for other commodities.

The Germantown glasshouse was burned in 1755, but was re-established by Jonathan Williams, who advertised its wares in the Boston newspapers. From these notices and from the evidence of recovered fragments, we find that the Quincy works made case bottles of various sizes, square and round bottles, snuff bottles, wide-mouthed jars for pickles and conserves, chemical vessels, and window glass. The business was still flourishing as late as July 1760.

Chapter three

∽∾∽∾∽∾∽∾∽∾∽∾∽∾∽∾∽∾∽∾∽∾∽∾∽

America's First Flint Glass

THE MANUFACTURE OF CLEAR GLASS TABLEWARE OF LEAD OR SODA metal was first attempted in the 1760's. Although chemical tests have proved that a large proportion of the so-called Stiegel glass is of soda-lime content, the credit for introducing flint glass should nevertheless be given to Henry William Stiegel. It is now thought that Stiegel's molded ware of English type was made of true flint metal by his English workmen, while his Continental-style engraved and enameled ware was of the soda glass with which his German glassmakers were familiar.

Stiegel was the first to produce clear and colored tablewares in competition with the English and Continental markets. He has achieved more fame than any other maker of American blown glass, and many colorful legends have grown up about him. Born in Cologne, Germany, Stiegel sailed for America in 1750, landing in Philadelphia. Although but twenty-one years of age, he was aggressive and self-confident. He soon found work with Jacob Huber, master of a pioneer iron works in Lancaster County. Within two years he had married Huber's daughter Elizabeth, thus acquiring a share in the business. Six years later, after his wife and her father had both died, he enlisted the interest and capital of some Philadelphia businessmen and thereafter ran the Elizabeth Furnace in his own name.

In spite of many stories to the contrary, Stiegel never had much money of his own. This circumstance did not, however, check him in an ambitious career. The reasons for his becoming a glassmaker can only be surmised. No doubt, since foreign importations of glass had become almost prohibitive in price as a result of the high English tariff placed upon them, the time seemed opportune for American competition. In

1763 he built a glasshouse at Elizabeth Furnace, which got under way in September of that year. In this factory were made bottles and window glass, and, it is thought, little more. Stiegel's intention was eventually to produce wares of a finer kind. Once his bottle works was established, he proceeded to the erection of another glasshouse at Manheim. Selling the products of his first venture to pay for the second, and borrowing money at every hand, he expanded in all directions.

Manheim was more than a glasshouse: it was a village of glassworkers and their families, with the mansion of "Baron" Stiegel, as he now permitted himself to be called, dominating the community. In truly baronial fashion, Stiegel supervised the activities of his workmen and the education of their children. He was especially concerned with their musical training, even leading a band that he had organized. His magnificently furnished and decorated manor house was the scene of lavish entertainments in keeping with the style of a man whose coach and four was ever ready for his journeyings abroad, and whose departures and arrivals were announced by the firing of a cannon.

When the new glass works began operations in November 1765, its owner was already entangled in a mass of debts. As the project met with some success, he became the more and more involved, and still he had not attained his objective. He found that, even with this new building, he was not equipped to turn out the glass of European style to which he aspired. For this greater ambition, a third and more pretentious establish-ment seemed necessary.

At some time before the erection of the Manheim factories, he had visited England, presumably to study methods and to secure a roster of workmen from Bristol and from Germany. The names of these glassmakers are known: we find among them English, Irish, and Germans, with a few Italians. In all, one hundred and thirty men, many of them trained in the best Bristol and German traditions, worked at the later Manheim glasshouse.

During the period from 1769 to May 1774, Stiegel gave to the world most of the objects of blown glass that bear his name. Although he had succeeded in his ambition, his own fantastic extravagances brought about his ruin. He borrowed from one source to spend in another until his finances were hopelessly undermined. In the fall of 1774, he was imprisoned for debt, and the "Baron" became plain Henry William Stiegel. After various activities as clerk and school teacher, following his release, he ended his days in the house of his wife's nephew at Charming Forge, where he died in 1785 and was buried in an unknown grave. His memory is kept green in Manheim by the annual "Feast of Roses." This began in the token payment of a red rose to Stiegel by the Lutheran Church as rent, in a ceremony accompanied by band music and gunfire. The occasion has been revived, with the rose presented to one of Stiegel's heirs.

Although a great deal of documentary evidence relating to the Stiegel output has been found, his wares are so similar to their English and German prototypes that positive identification of so-called "Stiegel" pieces is next to impossible. Students prefer to use the term *Stiegel-type*. Lists of the forms made at Manheim offer an imposing assortment of all the articles of tableware in vogue at the period. Decanters, flips, mugs, wine glasses, tumblers, syllabub and jelly glasses, sugar bowls, creamers, salts, cruets, candlesticks, smelling bottles—all these and many others are mentioned. Colors and types of ornamentation have been ascertained by Frederick William Hunter, author of *Stiegel Glass*, who conducted a series of excavations on one of the Manheim sites. He found that the clear glass is of a beautiful quality, with a smooth texture rarely equaled in English lead glass. It is frequently decorated by engraving or enameling. In contrast to foreign engraving, the Stiegel work was executed on thin blown glass and was left unpolished. Characteristic designs (Plate 5a) are several types of tulip, a basket of flowers, a sunburst with birds, wavy lines, rows of dots, and borders of intersecting arcs of circles filled in with lattice work. These motifs are presented in the simplified manner of a folk art, without any attempt at superior finish. In this respect they correspond to other Pennsylvania German arts. Engraving was applied to flips, tumblers, mugs, wine and jelly glasses, tea caddies and case bottles.

Painting with vitrifiable enamels was done at Manheim in the factory's closing years. It closely resembles work of the kind from Germany,

Switzerland, and France. According to Hunter, the Stiegel decorators used six brilliant opaque colors: white, yellow, a peculiar Nile green, light or dark cobalt blue, brick red, and black. The crudely executed designs are often of a floral nature, with some central motif such as a dove or other bird, a woman in a boat, a dog, or a building with a steeple. Mugs, tumblers, and drug bottles with pewter caps (Plate I) are the usual forms embellished in this manner.

More significant on account of its later influence on American glass is the use of pattern molds. Molding is one of the least expensive forms of decoration, but often the most effective, since the play of light through the varying thickness of the glass brings out the beauty of the material. When this quality is enhanced by free manipulation, which is by no means restricted when pattern molds are used, the most pleasing results are obtained. In pattern molding, the first gather of glass is blown into a part-sized mold, which gives an impression of ribbing, diamond design, paneling, or other marking. It is then withdrawn from the mold and expanded to any form desired by the glass blower. The expansion stretches the pattern so that it appears, not in rigid outlines, but as an indefinite impression. This work is most successful on colored glass, and it is in color that we find the best of the Stiegel pieces (Plate II).

Besides greenish glass in bottle colors, Stiegel produced rich blue, purple, amethyst, and emerald green. Blue or amethyst is most frequently seen, often in the form of sugar bowls, creamers, salts, and pocket bottles in expanded diamond design. The pocket bottle—a small rounded flask —is a typical Stiegel form, which is sometimes patterned with a daisy-like motif within a diamond or hexagon, combined with fluting (Plate 5b). The daisy bottles are distinctively American and almost unquestionably of Stiegel origin, as they have never been identified with any foreign or later American glasshouse.

Pattern molding was a part of the Bristol technique and it was certainly employed for inexpensive glasses in the northern English glasshouses. English creamers with straight or twisted ribbing were blown in blue or purple glass in the mid-eighteenth century, while clear flint examples of whorled ribbing date from an even earlier period. Although we feel that these patterned, hand-shaped objects have a primitive charm, in England such "peasant" glass is not highly regarded.

Impressions of sunken panels appear on rummers of clear glass, on flips, usually in combination with a band of engraving, and on blue, green, or amethyst vases (Plate 5c). Until recently these vases, which have rolled-over lips, have been accepted without question as being of Stiegel make, and it is indeed possible that some of them are the "blue flower jars" advertised by Stiegel. Molded paneling and rolled lips are, however, found on glass of a much later period. This is but one of many examples of continuing tradition in the glass industry.

It is obvious that much of the so-called Stiegel glass emanated from abroad or from later glasshouses at home. Mention should be made of an early flint-glass factory in Philadelphia, the Kensington works, which persisted under different managements until the middle of the nineteenth century. Founded in 1773, this concern a few years later advertised an extensive variety of wares, including cut glass, for household use. It is possible that it was the source of some of the Stiegel-type glass found in the Philadelphia area.

Not long after the temporary eclipse of glassmaking in Pennsylvania, a new enterprise appeared in Frederick, Maryland. This was the glass works of John Frederick Amelung, a native of Bremen, Germany, who, after many difficulties and delays, had brought to America a band of German workmen and had organized a company. At an expense of more than £23,000 he had built two glasshouses—the first completed in 1787, the second in 1790. His output was a fine quality of crown window glass and a variety of glass wares decorated by engraving in the best German style.

Since a number of specimens that can be authenticated by their engraved inscriptions have come to light, there is more definite information about Amelung's product than about any American glass of the eighteenth century. Although Amelung advertised that he made "flint glass," these pieces are all of soda-lime metal. Notable is a covered pokal in the Metro-politan Museum of Art (Plate 6a), which bears on one side the legend *New Bremen Glassmanufactory 1788—North America, State of Maryland,*

and on the other, *Old Bremen Success and the New Progress*, over the arms of the City of Bremen. A covered flip glass in the collection of Henry F. duPont is inscribed *Floriat Commercium*, above a wreath that encircles the name *Charles Ghequiere*; on the reverse is the identification *New Bremen Glassmanufactory the 20th of June, 1788.*

A third marked example, in the Garvan Collection at the Yale University Art Gallery (Plate 6b), is a flip glass with an interesting history. It was presented to the young son of John Phillips, first mayor of Boston, when he was sent as an emissary from the Boston Crown Glass Manufactory in 1789. The Boston company had not then begun operations, and it is probable that it was seeking advice and information in its untried venture of crown glass making. The inscriptions on this glass, with their characteristic floral embellishments, read: *Our best wishes for every Glassmanufactory in the United States. God bless the City of Boston.* and *Made at the Glassmanufactory of New Bremen in Maryland the 23 Jan. 1789 by John Fr. Amelung & Company.*

Other goblets, wines, flips, and bottles have been found with names, dates, or initials identifying them with Amelung's works. Characteristic of all are the soda metal of slightly greenish or smoky tone and the forms of German style. Notable is the reverse baluster stem of the pokals and goblets and the peculiar knobs on the covers.

The Amelung works was offered for sale in 1795. Visiting New Bremen a year later, the Duc de la Rochefoucauld-Liancourt said of it: "This manufacture has shared the fate of almost all first establishments of this nature, and is so near its destruction that that latter may be considered as complete."

After the failure of the Amelung enterprise, the workmen associated with it blazed new trails in glassmaking. A few, under the leadership of Albert Gallatin, the Swiss immigrant who became Secretary of the Treasury, went over the Alleghanies to found a glasshouse at New Geneva on the Monongahela River. Others joined with Amelung's son Frederick E. Amelung in an effort to establish the glass industry in Baltimore. Still others went to work in New Jersey, where so many of Stiegel's men had found employment.

Stiegel gave to America its first decorative tableware; Amelung produced the first glass of sophisticated type that could compare with the better glass made abroad. In the Stiegel wares we see the influence of both England and Germany; the New Bremen glass was purely Germanic in composition and execution.

Plate 7

CUT WINE GLASS

*This corresponds in design to glass exhibited by Bakewell & Company of
Pittsburgh at the Franklin Institute, Philadelphia, in 1825.
Bakewell won a prize for the best pair of cut decanters*

Plate 8

PITTSBURGH CELERY GLASS

*The heavy molded gadrooning and elaborate wheel engraving are found on
Pittsburgh pieces of the second quarter of the century*

〜〜〜〜〜〜〜〜〜〜〜〜〜〜〜〜〜〜〜〜〜〜

Chapter four

Flint Glass of the Early Nineteenth Century

AT THE TURN OF THE CENTURY, FLINT-GLASS MANUFACTURE WAS temporarily in abeyance and only glass for windows and bottles was being made. Fine glass was still imported from England and Ireland. Hundreds of thousands of drinking glasses alone were sent across the Atlantic every year from Cork, Dublin, Belfast, and Waterford. It was fully a quarter of a century before wealthy Americans, so accustomed to depend upon the British market, were ready to buy home-made tablewares. This state of affairs was brought about partly by the fact that the English manufacturers subsidized dealers in America in order to keep the market, until the tariff of 1824 made it possible for American glassmakers to undersell them.

For the re-establishment of the flint-glass industry in the early nineteenth century we are indebted to men of English descent. As early as 1807, a carpenter, George Robinson, and a glass man, Edward Ensell, began to construct a glasshouse in Pittsburgh, but were obliged to give up the enterprise for lack of funds. They were relieved by Benjamin Bakewell and his friend Benjamin Page, both from Derby, England, who brought the works to completion in the following year. This became the firm of Bakewell & Company, later Bakewell & Page.

Benjamin Bakewell has been called the "father of the flint-glass industry" in this country. It is noteworthy that he chose the frontier town of Pittsburgh for his works. Since the seaboard cities still preferred foreign glass, the west, whose communities could not easily obtain importations, offered better opportunity for sale. From the beginning, the Pittsburgh glasshouse was noted for quality and brilliance of its metal and for the splendor of its cutting. Cut glass of American manufacture was a novelty and as such attracted the attention of the whole country. Visitors from all over the world went to see the glassmaking at Bakewell's. Their unvarying enthusiasm is sufficient proof that we had at last succeeded in making luxury glass.

The authentication of specimens of cut glass is extremely difficult. Only where family tradition or other documentary evidence has preserved a record can we be sure of its origin. In 1824 and 1825 the Bakewells sent examples of their skill to the exhibitions of the Franklin Institute in Philadelphia, where they received honorable mention and then a reward for the best pair of cut decanters. If the history of these bottles were not known, it would be impossible to distinguish them from Irish glass of the period. The shape, the mushroom stoppers, and the strawberry diamond and fan cutting are all typical of contemporary Irish work. This same cutting appears as well on a fruit bowl with scalloped edge, and on mugs, tumblers, and wine glasses made in the same period (Plate 7).

A sugar bowl with identical cutting illustrates a change of form that took place in the early nineteenth century. Earlier bowls of Stiegel type have straight rims and flanged covers that fit inside them; later specimens were provided with curved brims and an interior ledge upon which their high-domed covers might rest. Although no date-line can be set for a style that evolved gradually, the second form, either with or without a high knopped or hollow stem and a foot, is typical of the Pittsburgh area.

The Bakewell firm had the longest continuous existence of any glass-house in the United States: it remained in operation until 1882. During those years it produced glass of every kind, although we are here interested only in its earlier products. In 1817 President Monroe ordered "a splendid equipage of glass . . . consisting of a full set of Decanters, Wine Glasses and Tumblers of various sizes and different models, exhibiting a brilliant specimen of double flint, engraved and cut by Jardelle, in which this able artist has displayed his best manner, and the arms of the United States on each piece have a fine effect."

Numerous examples with engraving in floral motifs, swags, or other conventional design, such as appear in Plate 8, have been with justice attributed to Pittsburgh, for it is quite certain that the Bakewells had artisans sufficiently skilled to execute the most elaborate decoration. A

Plate 9

a) PITTSBURGH VASE

The Stiegel-type molded paneling and rolled rim were still features of Pittsburgh blown glass in 1830

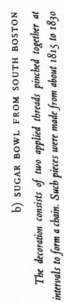

b) SUGAR BOWL FROM SOUTH BOSTON

The decoration consists of two applied threads pinched together at intervals to form a chain. Such pieces were made from about 1815 to 1830

Plate 10

a) CAMBRIDGE
BLOWN
MOLDED
SUGAR BOWL

Salts of similar
design are
known to have
been made by
the New
England Glass
Company in
the early 1820's.
This is a
unique attempt
to imitate the
form of china
sugar bowls

b) THREE-MOLD GLASS IN ARCH PATTERNS

The pitcher was blown in a pint decanter mold labeled Gin, *the mark being discreetly hidden under the handle*

famous example is a pair of flint-glass vases presented to Lafayette when he visited the works in 1825. These were engraved with the American eagle and a view of La Grange, home of the general.

Pittsburgh was destined to become the greatest center of the glass industry in the United States. Firm after firm was organized and one glasshouse after another constructed. Although a great deal of early glass is recognized as coming from this region, it is only in rare instances that it can be attributed to a particular maker. Much of it is not cut, but blown-molded, in the method first employed by Stiegel. Ribbed pattern molds were commonly used and the expanded diamond design persisted well into the nineteenth century. A band of sunken molded panels around the bases of fruit dishes, pitchers, sugar bowls, or celery holders is frequently seen on plain or engraved ware (Plate 9a). Characteristic compotes of this period have wide deep bowls that quite overbalance the small bases and knopped stems that support them. They are usually decorated by engraving in the Pittsburgh manner. A typical Pittsburgh form is a peculiar cruet with sharp spout pointing upwards, which is usually blown with straight or swirled molded ribbing. Some of the pattern-molded glass appears in rich tones of blue or amethyst, with occasional use of emerald green.

Inspired by the success of the Bakewell glass works, a group of Bostonians, who were already making window glass at Boston and Chelmsford, decided to try their luck at flint-glass manufacture. The War of 1812, with its interruptions of transportation and commerce, was bringing business almost to a standstill. Good glass could no longer be imported. This circumstance was the needed spur to American industry. In 1811, Thomas Cains, an experienced glass man who, as a child, had been trained in Bristol, arrived in Boston. As there was little for him to do in the crown-glass works, the Boston company leased to him part of a new but idle building which they had recently erected in South Boston. Cains built a small six-pot furnace and began blowing the first flint glass on the Atlantic seaboard. This was important, not so much for the glass he produced, as for its far-reaching effects in the establishment of other glasshouses.

In 1814, some of Cains's workmen left him to build a furnace in East Cambridge. This was the beginning of the great New England Glass Company, which was to become one of the largest glass manufactories in the world. Cains himself left the Boston company before 1820 to build a small factory of his own near by. Thus, in the 1820's, three concerns were running simultaneously in the vicinity of Boston, while a fourth was to be founded at Sandwich in 1825.

The early output of these eastern Massachusetts glasshouses represents a new element. Heretofore, in Boston, as at Pittsburgh, many of the glass-workers were German. The Massachusetts factories, however, were manned by workmen from England and Ireland, who made glass in the best traditions of the British Isles. They made a deliberate attempt to capture the British market, so long the source of fine glass used by New Englanders, and, in this endeavor, they were presently successful.

Cains turned out an astonishing variety of ware at his first little furnace. His 1816 advertisement mentions many articles that had not hitherto appeared on any American glass company's lists. Besides a long list of plain blown tableware, it notes goblets, finger bowls, sweetmeat baskets, cans (large mugs), barrel-shaped flips of several sizes, several kinds of lamps, inkstands, and a great variety of apothecary's and chemical ware. Cains practised cutting on goblets, wine and lemonade glasses, salts, and sugar bowls, and he embellished flips and tumblers with engraving. The only authenticated examples of early South Boston work now known are plain blown pieces with chain decoration formed by the application of two parallel threads pinched together at intervals (Plate 9b). This was a revival of an early eighteenth-century style of decoration.

From its beginning in 1818, when twenty-four cutting mills were installed, the cutting technique was emphasized at Cambridge, but the great mass of glass thus treated, because it cannot now be distinguished from imported ware, is lost to us. We must, therefore, consider some of the humbler aspects of glassblowing at this period. American industry, serving a democracy, has always been eager for money-saving short cuts. In glassmaking, they accomplished this objective by the use of molds, first for blowing and then for pressing.

As early as 1820, the Cambridge company was advertising "fan-end and octagon" molded salts. These were patterned in ribs and diamond point in imitation of cutting. They were heavy and thick, were blown in full-sized molds, and finished, not by hand manipulation, but by grinding the edges on the cutting machine after the pieces were annealed. Such salts are rather common, but other forms in this type of work are not. Round, oval, and eight-sided dishes are known. They were made at Cambridge, and probably also at South Boston, where molded plates and platters were advertised, and at Sandwich, where "oval molded dishes" were listed. Unique in such heavy glass is a sugar bowl of rec-tangular shape, following the style of a Staffordshire earthenware bowl (Plate 10a). This bears all the earmarks of Yankee ingenuity. By the very nature of hand manipulation, blown glass assumes a rounded form. Only by the use of a mold could it be brought to such an irregular shape. Its slumping lines and crudely finished edges show that this piece was made with some difficulty and probably as an experiment.

This clumsy method of molding was superseded by the simpler way of blowing thin glass into a full-sized mold and then working it into shape with tools. A whole category of beautiful glass thus made is now prized for its great variety and handsome patterns. Because it was blown in hinged molds that opened out in three sections to allow for safe removal of the glass, it is called *three-section mold,* or, more commonly, *three-mold* glass. Slight ridges or seam marks corresponding to the divisions of the mold may be detected on the finished ware. It may be noted that such seam marks have significance only on blown glass—never on pressed ware. Occasionally the molds were made in two or four parts, but glass of this category so made is still called "three-mold."

Three-mold glass is one of the few types that can with a fair degree of certainty be called American. Except for a very limited quantity of simply designed pieces from the Irish glasshouses, it was not made to any extent elsewhere in the early period. The first and simplest designs, illus-trated on page 52, were of geometric character composed of diamond diapering and fluting similar to the old heavy molding. At this stage it was but a substitute for cut glass, but it soon exhibited a style of its own.

The monotony of the early geometrical work was relieved by the addition of sunbursts, which were either rayed lines in a square or rectangle or were devised with bull's-eye or waffled centers. Designs of Gothic arches (Plate 10b) or cornucopias were blown at Cambridge before 1830, while at Sandwich, one of the most prolific producers of this ware, baroque patterns of arabesques carried this style of decoration far afield from the original imitations of cutting.

A great many different articles were created by this method. Among them are flips and other drinking glasses, pitchers of all sizes, sugar bowls, castor bottles, salts, bowls, deep dishes, toilet bottles, small lamps, and toy pieces. Few molds were needed to fashion all these forms. A tumbler mold could be utilized for a mug, an inkwell, a pitcher, or a hat; a decanter mold would do for pitchers, celery holders, and dishes. Such economy of method meant, however, that a good deal of hand manipula- tion would be needed to bring a piece to completion. In fact, the process of molding was but the initial step, establishing the pattern, in the shaping of objects by hand tooling. Pitcher rims, decanter necks, and bases re- quired hand work. In New England, pieces were often finished with threaded lips, and hollow blown handles are seen on larger ware. In blowing dishes, the bubble of glass was expanded after being removed from the mold, with a consequent softening of pattern that is most pleasing.

Three-mold glass was sometimes made in rich shades of amethyst, purple, blue, green, or even canary yellow, but such colors are com- paratively rare. Although some of the most beautiful colored ware has been identified with the Pittsburgh or Baltimore areas, it is thought that the greater number of artificially colored pieces derive from Massachusetts. Some three-section molds were used in bottle-glass houses at Keene, New Hampshire, in New York State, and in the middle west. At Keene, the forms were limited to decanter shapes and to inkwells, but the New York and Ohio glasshouses turned out bowls and pitchers and other offhand forms in green and aquamarine glass.

In 1825, Deming Jarves, who was the first manager of the New England Glass Company, left Cambridge to found his famous glasshouse at

Plate 11

a) TOOLED SUGAR BOWL FROM SANDWICH

The indentations were made by a pointed tool held against the vessel while it revolved. William E. Kern blew such pieces in 1829

b) CAMBRIDGE BLOWN SUGAR BOWL

Heavy pieces of this type, with molded gadrooning and applied threading below rim and on cover, were made by Thomas Leighton in the 1830's

Plate 12

a) EARLY BLOWN WHALE-OIL LAMP

The font is fluted in a pattern mold and the saucer has a folded foot. These first lamps appeared about 1815–25

b) WHALE-OIL LAMP OF THE 1820's

A hollow globular stem unites the blown font and square pressed base

Sandwich, Massachusetts. His reasons for building such an establishment in a remote village seventy miles from Boston seemed sensible at the time. In this location, wood for fuel, an endless supply of sand on the shore, and transportation by water were all at hand. Jarves kept his headquarters and salesrooms in Boston; his was never an isolated business.

The records of his early manufacture show that molded and pressed glass comprised a great part of it, along with plain blown ware that cannot now be identified. Occasionally some unusual offhand work of his early period comes to light. Some of these mementoes of Sandwich's past glory have been preserved in the museum of the town's historical society. In this category is the "bee-hive" sugar bowl in Plate 11a. This is almost the counterpart of another blown by William E. Kern in 1829 and is no doubt also an example of his work. The configuration of this piece was obtained, not by molding, but by tooling lines about it with sufficient pressure to indent them. It is an ancient technique that was practised in England soon after 1700 on the "terraced" feet of candle-sticks and other glasses. There are also American pitchers of this style, which have been expanded after tooling to give a wider spacing and shallower lines. With their tooled lips, hollow handles, and applied feet that form a vertical foot ring, they are delightful examples of a rare type of work. Shallow bowls, expanded after tooling until the markings are pleasingly indefinite, are likewise probably a Sandwich product.

Ornate banks were a favorite offhand *tour de force* at Sandwich. They were built up on bases into basket-like structures, fantastically trimmed with rigaree work and prunts and surmounted by hand-tooled birds. They were not, of course, peculiar to this one glasshouse, but represent the kind of plaything that skilled artisans liked to create as evidence of their dexterity.

Jarves's place at Cambridge was filled by Thomas Leighton, an Eng-lishman, formerly gaffer at Dublin and Edinburgh, who came here with five of his seven sons, all of whom were glassworkers in one capacity or another. This family, remaining in charge at Cambridge until 1874, exerted a profound influence on American glassmaking, and some of the pieces blown by them are among the finest examples of the art. Their work is characterized by the superior quality and high lead content of the metal, by its extreme weight, its simplicity of outline, and its careful finish. A type of blown ware associated with the Leighton name is illustrated in Plate 11b. This piece is of extremely heavy glass, especially thick in the lower section of the bowl, which was dipped into a second gather before the swirled gadroonings were shaped in a mold. Threadings appear below the rim and on the cover. This style of work was frequently adopted for presentation loving cups and other standing pieces, which generally had hollow stems enclosing coins. Similar vessels of this style were also made in other factories in the 1830's and have been found in the aquamarine color of window glass.

The Leightons in the early period introduced rich colors—notably blue, purple, emerald, green, and ruby. The latter was at first imported from England in lumps to be re-melted, but was after a time mixed here. William Leighton in 1848 devised the ruby formula for which the New England Glass Company was noted in the Victorian era. This ruby glass contained coin gold.

One of the most important branches of glassmaking during the first half of the century was the manufacture of glass lamps. Until after 1825, this was accomplished by blowing alone. The small, closed-reservoir whale-oil lamp had been introduced from England at the beginning of the century, gaining a popularity in America that it never attained abroad. By the time our flint-glass works were established, lamps of tin, brass, or silver were in common use. It was obvious that such a lamp made of glass would have many advantages in respect of cleanliness and beauty. The first glass lights were innovations devised by the glassblowers them-selves. They had no model for them other than the metal lamps and they were faced with the problem of fitting a burner cap where no screw thread could be provided. This difficulty they overcame by using a tight-fitting cork, upon which was attached a tin disc to hold the burners. The first glass lamps were probably the peg or socket type that could be inserted in a candlestick. They were advertised in the early 1820's. These were at first plain blown, but it was not long before they were ornamented with expanded ribbing or panel molding or by fine cutting or engraving. In

Plate III

SOUTH JERSEY VASE

*The striations in contrasting color are characteristic, and the ball cover
was a favorite decorative addition*

the three-mold period, a few were blown in geometrical or sunburst patterns.

The next step was to make a stand lamp. Relying upon traditional techniques, glassblowers made small lights with knopped stems and hand-tooled feet, exactly as they would shape a wine glass. Occasionally, they added a handle. These are known as *wine-glass* lamps. Tiny "spark" lamps first appeared as simple, bulbous forms; later, the shapes were heightened or small bases added. Curious indeed are the little Sandwich lights that were blown in a mold intended for a decanter stopper. Upside down, the hollow stopper makes a perfect spark lamp.

Larger specimens of the early period are among the finest and best-proportioned examples of early American glassblowing. They were provided with saucer bases to catch any drippings of oil. A few had fonts of dark blue glass to contrast with the clear saucer. The reservoir of the beautiful lamp in Plate 12a was blown in a pattern mold to give an impression of paneling. Saucer-based lamps with knopped stems may be attributed to South Boston, Cambridge, and Sandwich.

During the 1820's, a square molded foot of the kind seen on Irish glass was utilized as a lamp base (Plate 12b). Upon this foundation were built up, one above the other, hollow spherical sections and discs to make a high stem, the whole being surmounted by spherical, conical, or tall slender reservoirs. Lamps of this type were sometimes elaborated with cutting or engraving.

The early nineteenth century supplied many other more expensive lighting devices. Lustres for candles with cut stands and branches and hanging prisms were made wherever cutting was done. Splendid chandeliers, engraved globes for Astral lamps, lamp chimneys, and fancy panes or globes for hall lanterns were all included in this branch of glass-making, which was later to comprise the sole output of a number of glasshouses.

A great many glass works sprang up like mushrooms during and after the War of 1812, but, excepting Bakewell's at Pittsburgh and the establishments at South Boston and Cambridge, no other flint-glass manufactories were initiated before 1820. During that decade, a number of others were founded in New York, Brooklyn, Jersey City, Philadelphia, Baltimore, and Pittsburgh, and the manufacture of good American glass was assured. Rivalry to produce the finest glass or the best cutting was stimuated by the exhibitions of the Franklin Institute in Philadelphia and the American Institute in New York. Thus we find the Brooklyn Glass Works of John L. Gilliland being awarded a medal for the best flintglass ware at the third exhibition of the Franklin Institute in 1826 and the Jersey Glass Company receiving honorable mention for its cut glass. Gilliland had left the New England Glass Company in 1820 with Richard Fisher, with whom he built a glasshouse near what is now 47th Street and 11th Avenue in New York. Two years later he started a concern of his own in Brooklyn, both factories operating simultaneously. Workmen from Cambridge also founded the Union Glass Company in Kensington (Philadelphia). At Pittsburgh, Robert Curling and William Price, in their Fort Pitt Glass Works, and John Robinson of the Stourbridge Flint Glass Works offered serious competition to the old Bakewell firm.

In the years between 1820 and 1840, one hundred glass factories are known to have been in operation in the United States. All too little is known about these enterprises of a period when blown, handshaped flint glass was still the fashion, and only a few examples of their cut or molded wares have been authenticated.

THREEMOLD DECANTER
OF GEOMETRIC DESIGN

Plate 13

SOUTH JERSEY COVERED BOWL

The hand-tooled swan finial and petal base are typical of eighteenth-
and early nineteenth-century New Jersey techniques

Plate 14

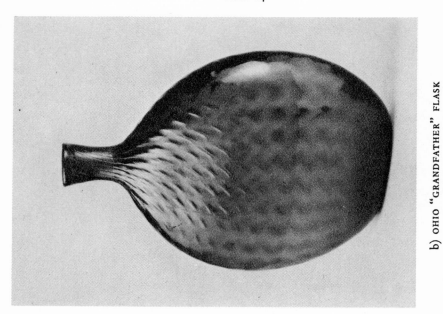

a) PITKIN FLASK

Bottles like this were double-dipped and patterned in a rib mold, then twisted to give the swirled effect. They date from about 1780 to 1820

b) OHIO "GRANDFATHER" FLASK

The broken swirl was produced by obtaining a rib impression in a pattern mold, followed by twisting and a second impression in another rib mold with subsequent expansion

Chapter five

The Bottle and Window-Glass Houses

VERY LITTLE AMERICAN FLINT GLASS MADE BEFORE THE INVENTION of the pressing machine was a truly native expression. It was a reflection of Continental and British design. The most original developments took place, not in the large flint-glass works, but in the country bottle and window-glass houses. In the offhand products of these establishments, the Wistar and Stiegel techniques were carried on to a late period in a traditional manner little influenced by more sophisticated glass work.

The bottle-glass houses had a tremendous rise in the early nineteenth century and many of them continued to function with the old hand methods as late as the 1870's. They were most numerous in New Jersey, New York State, New England, Ohio, and Pennsylvania. They pushed out to the frontiers of that time, in order to avail themselves of an adequate supply of wood and to supply small local markets with window panes and bottles, and, in some places, with vessels for household use. In New Jersey alone there were from time to time sixty glasshouses of this kind, and forty are known in New York State.

The products of these small factories almost invariably included wine bottles, demijohns, snuff and blacking bottles, inkwells, and such utilitarian ware. By 1820 many of them were putting out vast numbers of the typically American pictorial and historical flasks. More important than these regular manufactures was the output of individually created pieces made by the glassblowers, partly for presentation or for their own use, and partly for sale. Many of these articles, while following traditional patterns, exhibit so much ingenuity in the manipulation of the material that they rank with the highest art of glassmaking to be found anywhere. Although it is difficult to attribute glass of this kind to particular sources, it is sometimes possible to do so when it has a family or place history over a relatively short period.

The New Jersey glasshouses stemmed from the Stiegel and Wistar works. Jacob Stenger, a former Stiegel employee, was the first in this field when he established a business at Glassboro in 1781. From this enterprise, others arose. South Jersey glass, as it is called, displays certain features that may be recognized. It is almost invariably free-blown in bottle-glass colors, ranging in tone from green to amber, or in the aqua-marine of window glass, which in New Jersey has a slightly greenish tint. Blue, and more rarely amethyst, are also encountered. Occasionally a combination of two colors, such as aquamarine and amber, appears on one and the same piece. A type of decoration that originated in South Jersey, probably in the days of Wistar, is the *lily-pad* technique. To produce this effect, a vessel in the process of being blown is dipped into a second gather, which is then tooled by hand into a simple curved design suggestive of a lily-pad. Threading around the necks of pitchers and vases, and other applied ornamentation in the form of pinched or rigaree trailing, or prunts and seals, is commonly seen on New Jersey glass. Feet are often crimped. Covers of sugar bowls, otherwise plain, are sometimes embellished with a swan or other bird crudely fashioned by hand (Plate 13). Much of this Jersey glass is heavy and rather clumsy, having less instinctive balance of form than New York State pieces.

In the mid-nineteenth century and later, especially at Millville, a bi-color effect obtained by the fusion of threads of one color trailed in loops or striations upon another, was a favorite device. This method is illus-trated in Plate III. The basic glass is ordinarily aquamarine with lines of opaque white; less commonly a blue or amber groundwork is seen; while rose-colored striations appear in combination with white or other color. New Jersey forms include bowls, pans, pitchers, salts, lamps, vases, candlesticks, and many other objects designed for a particular need.

From New Jersey, glassblowers migrated to New York State, where they continued to blow offhand vessels with the same lily-pad technique. In fact, this type of work reached its peak in the window-glass factories of New York State. The brilliant aquamarine milk pans, bowls, compotes, pitchers, and sugar bowls blown at Redford, Redwood, Saratoga Mountain, and elsewhere are among the finest examples of the kind. At Lockport and Lancaster, lily-pad pitchers with threaded necks have been found in blue, while occasional pieces are of olive-yellow or amber. Amber, however, is a rare color in New York, as window-glass metal was usually employed. Since attribution has been made easier by the fact that most of the pieces have remained undisturbed in small communities, a wealth of unique examples from this area has been discovered and identified. Much of this glass is simple in character, but it is nevertheless sturdy in form and individual in design.

In New England, the Pitkin works at Manchester, Connecticut, near Hartford, was the first to be established after the Revolution. It was built in 1783 and ran until 1830. Generally attributed to this glasshouse is a type of flask with swirled ribbing known as a *Pitkin* flask (Plate 14a). A German influence is evident in these bottles, for they are blown by the "half-post" method of dipping into a second gathering of glass, so that the neck seems to be emerging from an outer coating. Although there is no definite proof that Pitkin flasks were made at the Manchester glass works, large numbers of them have been recovered in the vicinity of Hartford. Inkwells with swirled ribbing blown in the same manner are also considered a Pitkin type. It is obvious, however, that both flasks and inkwells emanated from various glasshouses: some of them must be attributed to Keene, New Hampshire.

Superimposed work in lily-pad style was done in New England at Stoddard, New Hampshire, by a blower who had gone there from New York, and at New London, Connecticut. The amber Stoddard pitchers and other heavy jars and vases are almost identical with known South Jersey pieces. A lily-pad pitcher on standard from New London is of aquamarine glass. Since both of these glasshouses were running in a late period, these pieces well illustrate the continuance of this tradition. Much beautiful offhand work was produced in other country glasshouses in New England. At Chelmsford, Massachusetts, and at Suncook, New Hampshire, fine pitchers, sugar bowls, plain bowls, and pans were fashioned of clear aquamarine glass, while many individual specimens have been preserved from the bottle houses in Westford, West Willington, and Coventry, Connecticut.

While little can be learned about the early midwestern glasshouses in what are now the large industrial centers, such as Pittsburgh and Wheeling, a great deal of information has been obtained about Ohio, largely through the excavations of the late Harry Hall White at Mantua and Kent. It would be impossible to mention the many industries of the kind that flourished in Ohio as soon as the land was settled. Enough has been gleaned from the stories of Kent, Mantua, and Zanesville to establish the fact that the Stiegel techniques were carried west in the early nineteenth century and there developed into richer and more purely American forms of expression in the wares of Ohio. Pattern molds were freely employed with new skill and adroitness. Pieces with rib impressions were often swirled or were even blown after swirling into another mold to get a second impression of ribbing across the first—the so-called *broken swirl* (Plate 14b). The expanded diamond technique was also utilized in the Stiegel manner. This work appears in the thinnest glass in brilliant shades of green and amber, or more rarely in blue or amethyst. Some of it is flint metal. Characteristic shapes are the bottles with globular bodies and slender necks, the bulbous, or flattened, rounded flasks, and the decanter-shaped bottles. Far more important than these is the quantity of table glass made in the small Ohio factories. Thin-blown and molded in the same fashion are creamers, sugar bowls, salts, bowls, small pans and dishes, compotes, cruets, and numerous other forms. It is with justice that these wares are given the highest rank in the whole range of early American glass manufacture. Their brilliant colors and pleasing shapes combine to constitute glass that has no need of extrinsic ornamentation. It was a product of the frontier, but a worthy one—the expression of glass men who had been trained in the country and who knew its needs.

While the shapes of table wares follow to some extent their Stiegel prototypes, some changes can be observed. Receptacles are generally somewhat larger. Many sugar bowls, especially those from Zanesville (Plate 15), have no foot or base. Their covers fit inside a flange and are domed or double-domed, while the body has its greatest diameter at the

Plate 15

AQUAMARINE MOLDED SUGAR BOWL

Attributed to Zanesville, Ohio, this piece illustrates the continuation of Stiegel techniques in the mid-nineteenth century. The high shoulder is typical of the Zanesville manner

Plate 16

a) OHIO THREE-MOLD BOWL

This corresponds in pattern to fragments unearthed on the site of a glass works in Kent, Ohio

b) HISTORICAL FLASKS

From left to right: Lafayette flask from Coventry, Connecticut, c. 1825. Portrait of Kossuth, Bridgeton, New Jersey, c. 1835–55. Success to the Railroad, Lancaster, New York, c. 1850

shoulder rather than, as in many Pittsburgh pieces, near the base. Some identified Mantua sugar bowls, however, have straight sides, with flanged covers and applied feet, thus more closely resembling Stiegel types.

Fragments of three-mold glass were found by Mr. White at Mantua and Kent. It is certain that all three of these centers made ware of this kind, but little of it has been identified. The rare pan in Plate 16a corresponds in pattern to recovered fragments. Its color is light green.

In the period between 1820 and 1860, bottle works in city and country turned out whisky flasks with symbolical or historical design. They are as American as anything we have in blown glass. Made in two-part molds, the early bottles were finished at the neck with little ado by whetting them away from the blowpipe and reheating the rims to smoothness at the glory hole. Later examples have rounded or flanged collars. Most of the bottles in this category were of a regular flask shape, somewhat bulging and with rounded contours in the early period, but later modified to a flattened form with straight tapering sides. Bottles of canteen shape or calabash type are also included in the list of American flasks. In the east their colors were as a rule limited to the natural greens and amber, but western flasks sparkle with the artificial hues of blue, green, or amethyst.

In American flasks we find reflected the history of a young country, which thus immortalized its celebrities and political events. Motifs like the American eagle or a horn of plenty were freely used, while the head of Liberty, agricultural symbols, or Masonic emblems made appeal to the public fancy. The head of Washington was a favorite motif. A Washington flask from Dyottville (Kensington), Pennsylvania, is marked *The Father of His Country* and *I Have Endeavour'd to do My Duty*. Lafayette appears on a number of bottles from different glasshouses. A Coventry, Connecticut, version made at the time of the opening of the Erie Canal shows him with De Witt Clinton. General Jackson and Zachary Taylor were popular subjects. One Taylor flask made at Baltimore reads: *Corn for the World*; another announces, *Gen'l Taylor Never Surrenders*. John Quincy Adams, Henry Clay, William Henry Harrison, and the visiting celebrities, Kossuth and Jenny Lind, are also portrayed.

Thomas W. Dyott, who produced great numbers of these whisky containers, was the only glassmaker who had the self-esteem to put his own visage on a bottle, and he placed it opposite that of no less a person than Benjamin Franklin. Dyott had come to America in 1795 as a poor boy. For some years he made and sold shoe blacking, then patent medicines, until, by 1812, he was calling himself "T. W. Dyott, M.D." It was but a step from the sale of nostrums to the manufacture of medicine bottles. In 1822, after acting as agent for a glass company, he was running the Dyottville Works at Kensington. His glasshouse was highly successful until he became involved in the financial panic of 1837, when he juggled the accounts in a bank he had founded and was, in consequence, convicted of "fraudulent bankruptcy." In spite of his notorious career, he was responsible for some of our handsomest bottles.

The coming of the railroad was celebrated on flasks, first by a design showing a horse-drawn vehicle on rails, and later by a crude engine (Plate 16b). Marked *Success to the Railroad*, these flasks are known to have been made at Coventry and at Lancaster, New York. A pictured steamboat with the legend *The American System* was another tribute to improved transportation.

Some of the most beautiful flasks were of irregular outline, somewhat like a violin in form, and were patterned with conventional scrollwork. They were made in the midwestern glasshouses of Pittsburgh and of Louisville, Kentucky, and in West Virginia. They are notable for their lighter and more brilliant blue, green, and amethyst tones. Flasks with sunburst design were made at Keene, Coventry, and Mount Vernon, New York. The Keene sunbursts are found not only in ordinary bottle colors, but also in deep bluish green, while Keene Masonic flasks display such rare hues as deep amethyst, violet blue, and green of all shades from a clear light color to nearly black.

As the historical flasks are often marked with the names of the glasshouses that produced them, many have been identified as to source and period. They are not so important for the craftsmanship displayed in their making as for being the record of an era.

Plate IV

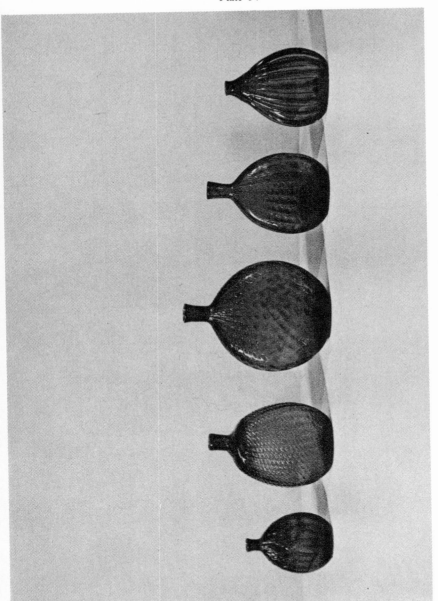

OHIO BLOWN FLASKS AND POCKET BOTTLES

The pattern molding of ribs and broken swirls is typical of Ohio glass craft

Chapter six

~~~~~~~~~~~~~~~~~~~~~~~~~~~~~~~~~~~~~

Pressed Glass

THE INVENTION OF THE PRESSING MACHINE, WHICH MADE POSSIBLE the quantity production of glass, created a revolution in glassmaking. It was the first major change of technique in nearly two thousand years. Bakewell of Pittsburgh, and the New England Glass Company were making knobs by this method in the early 1820's, but the first hollow vessel—a salt—was pressed at Cambridge in 1826. Other companies seized upon the idea and tried to improve upon it. In the following year, Phineas C. Dummer of the Jersey Glass Company obtained a patent for a mold with a core and a cover plate, called "Dummer's scallop." This device controlled the glass under pressure so that it could not escape over the edge of the mold. It was undoubtedly the clue that pointed the way to modern glass pressing.

At Sandwich, Deming Jarves had been pressing cup plates and other shallow ware, but no one had as yet produced a drinking vessel by mechanical means. In 1827, Jarves, assisted by a practical workman, succeeded in contriving a mold and a hand-operated machine by which he made the first pressed tumbler. Such a form must have required a hinged mold that could be opened for the removal of the finished vessel. By this simple invention he opened the way for the great wave of mass production that soon followed, bringing inexpensive glass into every home in the country. To the glassworkers, the prospect of a development that might rob them of their handcraft was frightening. They threatened Jarves's life, forcing him to remain inside his house for six weeks. Nevertheless, the new process was everywhere adopted and glassblowers still found work to do. The Jarves tumbler was still in existence in 1876, when it was exhibited at the Centennial Exposition. It was unfortunately broken at that time, but a surviving drawing shows its pattern of bull's-eyes and scale between pillar flutes.

The use of elaborately designed molds gave the early output at Sandwich a unique distinction. Much of it belongs in the category of so-called *lacy glass*—a term suggested by the lacy appearance of the groundwork, which is covered with fine stippling. Lacy patterns are eminently suited to the pressing process, for they are not imitations of cutting or engraving, but are designs that could be obtained by no other technique. For two decades glass of this kind was produced in great quantities at Sandwich, Pittsburgh, and elsewhere. It was eventually abandoned on account of the expense of mold-making and simpler designs were substituted.

Much of this early pressed ware was in the form of flat or shallow articles, although sugar bowls, pitchers, compotes, celery holders, and even covered dishes were successfully attempted. Cup plates, tea plates, sauce dishes, and salts comprised the bulk of the output. The greater part of it was pressed in clear lead glass, which, contrary to the general impression, was not of fine quality, but was full of bubbles and lumps of unfused quartz, besides having an unpolished and uneven surface resulting from the pressure of the plunger.

Lacy glass design was so contrived as to cover the entire surface of a dish, leaving no blank spaces. If a suffocation of ornamentation resulted, the general effect was still one of sparkle and extreme brilliance calculated to appeal to a public that had been accustomed to the plainest of blown glass. In lacy molds we see many elements of Empire design that were commonly used in other media in the eighteen-thirties. The lyre, acanthus leaf, lotus flower, cornucopia, and basket of flowers appear on early nineteenth-century furniture, the peacock feather on contemporary cut glass, while pointed arches bespeak the period of the Gothic revival. These motifs were placed in unrelated combinations, often with fields of pressed diamond point or strawberry diamond in imitation of cutting. Such naturalistic motifs as thistles, acorns and oak leaves, roses, eagles, or ships were introduced against stippled backgrounds in juxtaposition with borders of acanthus, palmettes, peacock feathers, or other conventional design.

Plate 17

CONVENTIONAL AND HISTORICAL CUP PLATES

The Ship Chancellor Livingston, *Fort Meigs, and portrait of Henry Clay
reflect events of the 1830's and 1840's*

Plate 18

a) UNIQUE MIDWESTERN
CREAMER

The mark R. B. Curling & Sons
Fort Pitt *on this fine lacy pitcher
establishes the skill of western
glassmakers in adopting lacy design*

b) WASHINGTON-LAFAYETTE
SALT

*One of the earliest examples of pressing,
this crudely molded salt faintly shows a
bust of Lafayette on one side and that of
Washington in a medallion on the other*

Even earlier than these lacy types was a small group of pressed dishes that had simple backgrounds of strawberry diamond and borders of hearts or fans combined with lyre, sheaf of wheat, or other small motifs. Such ware is often thick and sometimes misshapen, as pressers had not thus early acquired sufficient skill to gather the exact quantity of glass needed to fill a mold.

As lacy glass was left unpolished just as it came from the mold, its rims, usually serrated or scalloped, are sharp to the touch. A characteristic midwestern treatment is a series of small lobes, each containing a tiny bull's-eye. Similar bull's-eyes also occur in the groundwork of some Pittsburgh glass, where they are utilized as a foot rest for the dish and thus are made a structural part of it. Sandwich and other eastern lacy glass rests on a foot ring. Some early plates and cup plates have a narrow rope edge in place of serrations. Relief design on both upper and under surfaces occasionally appears on pieces of this type.

By the early eighteen-thirties, lacy glass was being pressed in all forms. During the next two decades the manufacturers, following the trend of the era, introduced historical and commemorative patterns. An early example is the oval dish with eagles and ships that are supposed to represent the *Constitution*. Washington is seen on an amusing Sandwich tea plate, which, by an error of the moldmaker, is marked *Washington George*. A so-called "Industry" dish was brought out at the time of Harrison's presidential campaign in 1840. It shows a log cabin, a man with a plow, a sailing ship, and a glasshouse—the latter a view of the New England Glass Works. Although this plate must have originated at Cambridge, there are several versions of it that were doubtless made elsewhere. A notable midwestern dish on page 16 is octagonal in form, and bears the representation of a side-wheel steamer. It has the typical bull's-eye rim.

By far the greater number of patriotic and historical subjects appear on cup plates (Plate 17). These little objects, which were about three inches in diameter, were employed as a rest for the tea cup while tea was drunk out of the saucer. Sold for a few cents apiece, they retained their popularity for thirty years or more. Hundreds of them were adorned with charming conventional or lacy patterns, a few had portrait heads of Washington or Queen Victoria, while such lesser celebrities as Henry Clay, Harrison, or Major Ringgold of Palo Alto fame appeared on others. Views of steamships, such as the *Chancellor Livingston* or the *Benjamin Franklin,* which were running on the New York–Providence line before 1834, of Bunker Hill Monument, or of the log cabin and cider barrel of the Harrison campaign reflected popular enthusiasms of the time. Various types of eagles symbolized the pride of a growing nation. Cup plates are found in clear glass and in a wide range of colors. There is evidence that they were made in all the early factories that adopted the pressing process.

Early pressed salts are found in almost endless variety. As a rule, they are rectangular, boat-shaped, or basket-shaped, with feet or bases; a few are circular. The forms are dictated by the intricate lacy designs. Several of the earliest have no stippling, but are rather plain box-like shapes with serrated rims and columns at the corners. In this category is the exceedingly rare Washington and Lafayette salt illustrated in Plate 18b, which has a bust of Washington in relief against a clear ground on one side and the head of Lafayette in an oval panel on the other, each with a faint impression of the names. Another interesting historical example displays on the base a picture of an early steam engine and car over the name *H. Clay.*

A number of the first salt dishes were marked with factory and place names, with the evident purpose of advertising the skill and enterprise of the manufacturers in the use of a new process. One, made in both clear and light-green glass, is marked *Jersey Glass Co. Nr. N. York.* It closely resembles the Washington-Lafayette salt in shape and is simply decorated with a basket of flowers on each side and a wild rose motif on the ends. Almost identical is the marked salt from Cambridge, which is lettered *N.E. Glass Company Boston.* This is found in clear or opalescent glass, or, rarely, in blue. At Sandwich the marked salt was pressed in the form of a side-wheel steamer, with the word *Lafayet* on the side and *B. & S. Glass Co.* on the stern (page 83). The designation *Sandwich* also appears on the interior and on the base of some examples. These little boats were made in opaque white or light blue, in sapphire blue, canary yellow, or opalescent glass. A better designed and executed boat was

Plate 19

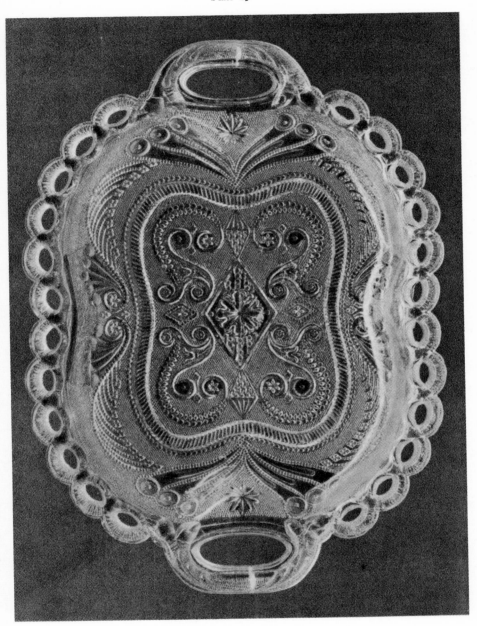

SANDWICH LACY TRAY

The open handles and border design represent the epitome of early pressing technique at Sandwich

Plate 20

a) PATTERNS OF THE CIVIL WAR PERIOD

*How design became progressively more elaborate is shown in these pieces
of bellflower, pineapple, and inverted fern*

b) WASHINGTON PATTERN BOWL, C. 1840–1860

*Early pattern glass was designed in imitation of contemporary cutting.
This pattern bowl has been treated with acid on the under surface
to produce a "moonstone" coloring*

Plate 21

a) EARLY CAMBRIDGE LAMP

*Lamps of this type appear in various opaque colors
and are sometimes marked* N. E. G. Co.

b) LAMP WITH CUP PLATE BASE

*Lacy cup plate molds were utilized in the 1820's
to make attractive feet for lamps*

Plate 22

a) BLOWN CANDLESTICK
WITH PRESSED BASE

Probably made before 1820, this illustrates the ineptitude of the glassblower in designing a nozzle that would catch the drip

b) SANDWICH DOLPHIN CANDLESTICK

The dolphin, a common motif of the 1850's, is here combined with petal sockets frequently seen with other bases

turned out by the Robinsons at Pittsburgh. Marked either *Pittsburgh* or *J. Robinson & Son Pittsburgh*, it has been found in rich blue and amethyst as well as in clear glass. Still another salt, which has been the subject of some controversy, is labeled *Providence*. It has been attributed to Sandwich, but it is almost certainly a similar advertising piece from the Providence Flint Glass Company, of Providence, Rhode Island, which was organized in 1831 and is known to have made pressed glass. An eagle cup plate with the words *Fort Pitt*, a plate with the Robinson mark, and a creamer stamped *R. B. Curling & Sons Fort Pitt*—all from Pittsburgh—were also put out to identify their makers with the pressing process. The creamer (Plate 18a) is similar to some Sandwich examples, but is important for establishing the use of fine lacy design in a midwestern glasshouse. All such marked pieces are indication of the eagerness with which manufacturers all over the country pushed the new mechanical methods of glassmaking.

Among the larger and more ambitious forms of lacy type may be mentioned the trays with open handles (Plate 19) and the rectangular compotes on high foot that occur in canary yellow, deep blue, peacock blue, amethyst, and bluish green. Their rarity suggests that colored lacy glass was not produced in quantity. In fact, the designs appear to far better advantage in clear glass. Octagonal or rounded sugar bowls with patterned covers were made in numerous glasshouses and in rich colors. Gothic or acanthus designs predominate in these pleasing containers.

In addition to the lacy designs, simpler patterns of fluting in imitation of cut glass were also being made in the 1830's. The first pressed goblets—a form not attempted in American lacy glass—were made in this style. The following decade saw the beginning of the great mass production of pattern glass, which flooded the country during the next forty years. The term *pattern* in this connection means a whole matching set of glass ware. It includes a sugar bowl, creamer, spoon holder, butter dish, celery vase, plates, salts, round and oval nappies, goblets and wine glasses, egg cups, and other pieces. Much of this glass is interesting as reflecting the taste of the mid-Victorian era.

The first patterns were simple flutes, prisms, and diamond points, adapted from motifs used in cutting (Plate 20b). A vast deal of hand labor was expended on these earlier wares. Lips were shaped by hand and handles separately made and applied while the glass was hot. A smooth, lustrous surface approximating that of blown ware was obtained by reheating during manipulation. Known as *fire-polishing*, this process was accom‑ plished by attaching a pontil rod to the vessel and thereby presenting all possible surfaces to the flames of the glory hole. The pontil marks were afterwards ground out. Their presence on pressed glass does not indicate that blowing played any part in its manufacture.

New short‑cuts in ways of pressing soon reduced this hand work to a minimum. As this occurred, designs were elaborated (Plate 20a). Ribbed patterns, with the addition of bellflowers, ivy, or grapes, and conven‑ tionalized motifs such as the New England pineapple, tulip, horn of plenty, or bull's eye and fleur‑de‑lis, appeared in the Civil War period. All this glass was rather heavy and of good quality.

Color was sparingly used in the earlier pressed tableware. Opalescent and canary yellow ("gold color") or cobalt blue have been encountered on occasional pieces, while translucent white, turquoise blue, jade green, or lavender appear on a few rare Sandwich egg cups and spoon holders.

In the 1860's, William Leighton at Wheeling devised a formula for soda‑ lime glass that was well suited to the pressing process. All the western glass‑ houses adopted it, while the New England manufacturers continued to make flint glass only. Lime glass does not have the weight or resonance of lead metal, nor does its surface have the soft texture that simulates blown glass. To obviate its deficiencies, more ornate patterns of naturalistic floral, fruit, or animal character were created and a series of new colors was intro‑ duced. A great deal of the pressed glass of the 70's and 80's is found in amber, light canary‑yellow, greenish blue, and apple‑green. These hues have no depth or beauty of tone and were employed for the manufacture of the cheapest wares and for ornamental gadgets.

A pleasing Centennial period glass made by the Gillinders of Phila‑ delphia combines clear metal with acid‑finished design or motifs resem‑ bling camphor: hence the term *camphor* glass. The best known of these wares is *lion* glass, knobbed and decorated with camphor lions, and the

Plate 23

CASED TOILET BOTTLE

*This bottle, cased with sapphire blue over clear glass, exemplifies the elaborate
hand work done at Cambridge in the 1850's*

Plate 24

a) SILVERED GLASS VASE

An elaborate example of engraving on blown silvered glass, this is one of the better examples in an inartistic category

b) MEDALLION PAPERWEIGHT

Weights of hexagonal shape impressed with likenesses of historic personages were put out at Cambridge in the 1850's

c) MILLEFIORI PAPERWEIGHT

Cased with red over opaque white over clear glass, this piece represents the epitome of skilled workmanship in paperweight art. Formerly owned by William Leighton of Cambridge and Wheeling, it is attributed to the New England Glass Company

Westward Ho pattern. The latter (Plate 25) shows a log cabin, a bison, and a deer in a scene that encircles each piece. It was obviously a bid for the western trade.

One of the most important branches of glass pressing was the manufacture of lamps. Its earliest application for this purpose seems to have been in the addition of lacy bases to plain blown fonts. Some of these bases were pressed in molds made for the purpose, but others, like the one in Plate 21b, were shaped in cupplate molds. The cupplate bases were made rather thick and heavy and were used upside down, the pressed design being left uppermost. Whether attached directly to the reservoir or joined by means of a knopped stem they make a suitable and decorative standard.

Later lamps had fonts freeblown or blown in molds, with pressed bases united to them while both were hot. Perhaps the earliest of this type is the one illustrated in Plate 21a, which stands on a hollow plinth with lion'shead corners. Its simple design of a basket of flowers against a plain ground is reminiscent of the early pressed salts from the New England Glass Company. It is, therefore, not surprising to learn that examples of this lamp have been found with the mark *N E G CO.* on the interior of the base. The globe is original and exemplifies the correct type for early whaleoil lights. This lamp must have been made in quantities, for, although it belongs to the period before 1830, it is not extremely rare. It has been found in clear and opalescent glass, in opaque white, and in opaque lavenderblue. Fonts vary, and may be globular, pearshaped, or tapering. Other lamps with numerous types of stepped bases were common in the 1830's.

Eventually entire whaleoil and camphene lamps were made in separate parts in the pressing machine and united as they were released from the molds. Thousands of styles were created, for the whaleoil lamp almost wholly superseded the candle in America. In the 1850's, it was described in an English report as being "peculiar" to the country. The glass lamp was indeed a clean, attractive light, well designed and fitted for its intended use. Although rare examples are found in rich shades of blue, green, amethyst, and canaryyellow, the greater number of such lamps are of clear glass.

In the later output of kerosene lamps, the large globular oil fonts were usually blown in molds, while the bases were pressed, the parts being connected with brass collars. The square or cyma-curved feet were often jet-black or opaque white. At Sandwich, where lamps were a major part of the manufacture in the 70's, opaque or translucent pastel colors were used in great variety. Lines of gilding were sometimes added to produce an "elegant" effect.

Few candlesticks, except for occasional offhand examples from the bottle and window-glass factories, were made in America before the advent of pressing. Thereafter, they appear in numerous styles and are among the more interesting objects shaped with the assistance of the machine. The earliest are, however, largely the product of hand labor. The first of them seem to have had pressed bases only, with stems and nozzles free-blown. Of this type is the one in Plate 22a, which is built up with hollow knops and wafers above the old-fashioned square pressed or molded foot. Oddly enough, the rim is turned down rather than up, with disregard for the fact that melting wax would drip from it instead of being retained. In this respect it is unique. Identified Pittsburgh candlesticks have proper sockets above knopped or hollow baluster stems, which sometimes rest upon spreading feet patterned in the hairpin design of cup plates. Several types of stepped bases in square, quatrefoil, or cloverleaf shape were combined with plain blown or lacy sockets in many ingenious combinations. Horizontally ribbed knops often connect lacy sockets with hollow molded stems, and knops or wafers of glass usually appear at the junction of stem and base. A fine octagonal lacy base or a scrolled tripod with lion's feet is also seen in conjunction with lacy sockets.

As pressed glass ceased to be a novelty and means of eliminating hand work were sought, candlesticks became rather simpler affairs in point of construction. Hexagonal columnar sticks pressed in one operation were turned out at Cambridge before 1850. Of unimaginative design, they depended for their appeal upon unusual color, such as red amber, emerald-green, royal purple, sapphire-blue, canary, opalescent, opaque white, or almost transparent alabaster. Hexagonal candlesticks from

Plate 25

WESTWARD HO COVERED COMPOTE

The Indian, bison, and log cabin were motifs calculated to capture the western trade.
Westward Ho was made by Gillinder & Company of Philadelphia

Plate 26

a) PEACHBLOW WATER PITCHER

*One of several wares originated
at Cambridge in the 1880's, peachblow is
a shaded glass with mat surface. Its luscious
color flows from rose red to warm white*

b) EXAMPLES OF "BURMESE" GLASS

*Emanating from the Mt. Washington Glass Company in New Bedford, Massachusetts,
this ware was often blown in excellent form. Its color ranges from
coral pink to lemon yellow*

Sandwich were pressed in two or three parts and united by wafers of molten glass.

Most famous of candlestick designs is the dolphin. It probably made its first appearance in the 1850's in response to the rise of Venetian influence in glassmaking. The larger varieties on single or double square bases (Plate 22b) are of Sandwich origin. With hexagonal or petal sockets, they were pressed in the whole gamut of Sandwich clear, translucent or opaque colors, or sometimes in combinations of color, such as alabaster and translucent blue. Other plainer candlesticks with the same sockets were made with flaring hexagonal or petal-patterned feet. The McKee brothers at Pittsburgh produced dolphin candlesticks that had six-sided or scalloped circular bases. In the 1860's they turned out pretty little sticks supported by small dolphins on petticoat bases. These were of lime glass in light peacock-blue or canary with opalescent rims.

By the mid-nineteenth century, the manufacture of glass by machine methods had come to stay. As a result, the mass of people, who could not afford hand-made wares, could have attractive and useful glass in their homes. Such glass is widely collected today for its sentimental and antiquarian interest, but it should not be confused with the creations of early skilled glass-blowers.

BOAT SALT FROM SANDWICH

〜〜〜〜〜〜〜〜〜〜〜〜〜〜〜〜〜〜〜〜〜〜〜〜〜

Chapter seven

Victorian Blown Glass

IN SPITE OF THE ENORMOUS QUANTITIES OF AMERICAN PRESSED glass made for home consumption and for export to our own frontiers, to the West Indies, and to Europe, the art of blowing glass still flourished in the Victorian era. There were always customers for the more expensive hand-made articles. The taste of the mid-nineteenth century demanded solidity and size and a great deal of elaboration in the form of cutting, engraving, and gilding. In fact, glass wares were imposing. Fruit dishes, compotes, and epergnes of extraordinary height made an impressive array on the table, while vases and chandeliers suited to the high-ceiled rooms of the time gave a desired effect of magnificence.

At this period the New England Glass Company at Cambridge, Massachusetts, surpassed all others in purely technical accomplishment. In its workrooms glassblowers from England and Ireland created a multitude of forms, while craftsmen from Germany brought the Continental art of engraving to its highest development in this country. A contemporary writer, who visited the Cambridge glasshouse in 1852, said of it: "We were repeatedly struck with the fact, new to us, that most of the exquisite, richly colored and decorated glass ware, which is so much admired under the name of 'Bohemian Glass,' is manufactured at these works." American glass decorated in this style differed from the foreign ware in being blown from the finest flint metal. Casings of color over clear glass were cut and engraved as in Plate 23, to produce the well-known Bohemian effects, while clear drinking glasses, decanters, and other table wares were covered with wheel engraving in naturalistic designs. As early as 1850, the Cambridge company was making toilet bottles and lamps cased and cut away to show the underlying surface in such colors as blue, ruby, pink, emerald-green, olive, and mulberry. These were further garnished by engraving on the cut portions and by gilding. After the introduction of kerosene lighting, this technique, popularly known as "overlay," was also practised extensively at Sandwich, where large lamps were thus ornamented on font, column, and globe.

Engraving on clear glass reached a high point of technical excellence in the period from 1840 to 1860. Designs were for the most part realistic. Hunting scenes and similar compositions showing animals, trees and foliage were incised deeply in heavy metal to give an appearance of bold relief when seen through the glass. Engravers made their own drawings for this ornamentation, which usually bore little relation to the form of the vessel to be decorated. Toilet bottles, goblets, pitchers, compotes, and other table utensils of this type are valued not so much as works of art as for the skillful execution of the engraving.

Following a change of taste after the Civil War, glass to be engraved was blown paper thin and covered with the most delicate tracery of grape or ivy vines. Venetian rather than Bohemian influences dictated the forms, which were intended to convey an impression of lightness. Exceedingly slender straw-stem wines took the place of the heavy baluster-stemmed glasses of the preceding decades, while ewer-shaped or long-necked decanters supplanted the stolid bottles of the 1850's. The thin metal of much of this glass precluded any deep intaglio engraving, and the art soon degenerated to the point where its shallow incising could be imitated by the cheapest acid etching.

This was the period of the bowl or dish on foot—the Italian *tazza*— and of the epergne. The latter, made in sections, was a complicated affair that sometimes attained a height of two feet or more. In its simplest guise, it consisted of a shallow dish with a trumpet-shaped vase rising from a socket in the center. In more elaborate style, the saucer was elevated on a standard, while the central vase was surrounded by other smaller ones interspersed with glass leaves or by a series of curved arms holding glass baskets. These imposing centerpieces were a specialty at Sandwich, where the flower-holders were often engraved in fern design or were blown of opalescent or other colored glass. The rope twisting of the arms, the ruffled rim of the vases, the tooled leaves, and the dolphins that sometimes upheld these compositions were all rather clumsy imitations of Venetian techniques. Fine threadings of color on clear glass were likewise inspired by Venetian work. In America, however, this application of glass thread, since it was not entirely accomplished by hand, displayed a certain mechanical rigidity. Furthermore, the glass itself was sometimes shaped by pressing. Blown bottles and finger bowls in this style are frequently seen entirely covered with threads of blue or pink, while other pieces have lines of matching color.

Cutting in the early Victorian days was executed in the simplest manner, appearing as flutes, prisms, or circular "printies" or "punties" on heavy decanters, drinking glasses, and pitchers. In fact, ornate cutting was neglected in favor of engraved design. The technique was revived at the time of the Centennial Exhibition in 1876, when the manufacturers introduced table glass that was literally covered with all the cutting it could bear without breaking. The brilliance of this work made a sudden appeal to the popular fancy, with disastrous results in the later years of the century.

Among the tremendous number of things fashioned for the glass trade in the mid-nineteenth century, millefiori paperweights held an important place. Made up of sections of colored rod or bits of hand-made flowers, leaves, or fruit encased in a hemisphere of crystal glass, they display infinite variety and ingenuity. Paperweights were introduced here in the 1840's by men like François Pierre and Nicholas Lutz, both of whom had been trained in France, and they were put out by all the large flint-glass houses. They are largely individual productions, depending for their beauty on the skill of the maker in arranging his colors and patterns.

The creation of millefiori weights was not as mysterious a process as it appears. First of all, a gather of hot glass was dropped into a hemispherical mold, which would form the upper surface of the finished piece. The bits of color, previously cut from prepared rods, were heated to softness in the flame of a "lamp," or blow torch, and were then speedily arranged on the clear glass in the mold. This done, another gather of hot metal was added to cover them, and the whole tipped from the mold. Polishing and grinding to obtain a smooth surface completed the process.

Some of the best millefiori examples are cut in large flutes, which show the design as if through little windows and at different angles. A few were made of colored glass or were cased with blue or red over opaque white before cutting. The specimen in Plate 24c was formerly owned by William Leighton and was made by a member of his family. Numbers of American paperweights appear with clusters of fruit or various flowers against latticinio backgrounds of white spirals.

Of American origin, also, are weights in the shape of apples, pears, or other fruits. They are usually shaded in color from red to yellow and rest on clear bases. In the 1850's, the New England Glass Company made medallion paper-weights (Plate 24b). These are hexagonal blocks of flaw-less crystal, through which appear in seeming relief busts of Clay, Webster, or other celebrities. The heads are so sharply impressed that they seem to be the result of hand engraving, but, as they are found duplicated in every detail, it is obvious that they are made by mechanical means.

A curious Victorian novelty was silvered glass, for which the New England Glass Company secured a patent as early as 1855. This was a showy, but clumsy and inartistic, product in imitation of silver, which, nevertheless, had a tremendous popularity in its day. In its original mani-festation, it appeared in forms suited to the technique, such as curtain pins, furniture and door knobs, and gazing globes, but its later adaptation to tableware was extremely inept. Silvered glass was blown double and coated on the interior with a silver nitrate preparation. It was then subjected to a baking process, the surplus liquid removed, and each article carefully stopped with cork coated with resin, or, at Cambridge, with glass plugs made to fit. Although knobs and globes, being naturally hollow, were but single bulbs of blown glass, they, too, had to be sealed to prevent contact with the atmosphere, which caused the silvering to deteriorate. Some of this glass was perfectly plain, but the itch for decoration led to the addition of engraved design (Plate 24a) and even to painting in colors.

Silvered glass was made in different factories and varies greatly in quality, some of it being paper thin and poorly silvered, while other specimens are of strong, heavy, lead glass. Vases, candlesticks, paperweights, sugar bowls, pitchers, goblets and salts were among the many objects so made during the score of years when this ware was in vogue.

In the 1880's American glassblowing, in both form and color, ran riot. A revolution against the cold classicism of the Greek revival period and the ensuing dreary pseudo-Gothic seemed to have got under way. This change was undoubtedly brought about by a new acquaintance with the art of other countries as seen at the Centennial Exhibition. The influence of Oriental ceramics is especially noticeable in the efforts to make "art glass." The results were not always admirable, for they denied the true function of glass—to transmit light. Opaque colors and mat surfaces obtained by the use of an acid bath were among the common devices that made glass look like something different from what it was. Porcelains and even metals were imitated. Glassmakers were perhaps a little addled by the fact that they had learned how to produce glass in any wanted color or combination of colors. Color is indeed the keynote of the last quarter of the century. Shapes are marked by irregularity, or even asymmetry, and pinched or ruffled edges are common. However, a few vases blown in exact replica of Chinese ceramic forms present a welcome relief from the unorganized styles of this era.

Although all the factories that made blown wares participated in the creation of new effects, the wares of Cambridge, Sandwich, and Wheeling are the best known. At Cambridge, and at the Mount Washington Glass Company in New Bedford, Massachusetts, colored glass shaded by reheating was devised. *Peachblow* and *amberina* are familiar examples of this type of work. The peachblow, or wild rose, of Cambridge (Plate 26a) runs from opaque white to deep rose, and the New Bedford ware of the same name shades from a faint blue to rose pink. Both of these are homogeneous glass, without a lining, and are generally seen with an acid finish. The peachblow of the Hobbs, Brockunier Company at Wheeling ranges in color from light yellow to red and is cased over a white lining, which gives it an opaque appearance. The term *peachblow* was suggested by a famous Chinese peachbloom vase that was auctioned for a large sum in the early 1880's. The Wheeling company made an exact copy of the form of this vase, even including its three-legged stand of pressed amber glass. Amberina is a transparent flint glass, often blown in molds that give an uneven surface, and running in color from a pale amber to rich ruby. It was first made at Cambridge and at New Bedford, where it was called *rose amber*. The *Burmese* of New Bedford (Plate 26b) is a similar glass, usually with dull finish, that shades from yellow to coral pink. In its day it was considered the most attractive of these colored wares. A set made for Queen Victoria so captivated her that an English glasshouse made arrangements for the use of the American patent rights in order to manufacture it in England. Unfortunately, much Burmese of otherwise good design was marred by the addition of enameled flower sprays, birds, or even verses of poetry. It is interesting to note that none of the glass with mat finish, excepting perhaps this Burmese, which has been revived had any lasting popularity.

At Wheeling mineral flakes were incorporated with glass to give a gold or silver spangled appearance and a crackled surface was produced by subjecting glass to sudden changes of temperature. Sandwich and other glasshouses, by rolling a gather of opaque white in a mixture of glass fragments of assorted colors, which fused with it, made an extraordinary variegated coloring for vases and baskets. A mottled ware imitating tortoise-shell was also a novelty of this period. Blown vases of clear, colored, or striped glass with realistic flowers and leaves cut out and applied to them perhaps represent the apogee of the bric-à-brac era.

A distinguished creation of the 1890's was the *Favrile* glass of Louis Comfort Tiffany. This artist, after a period of experimentation with color for windows and other structural glass, established a factory at Corona, Long Island, and devoted himself to the production of individually designed pieces of unique style. His admiration for the coloring and iridescence of ancient glass long buried led him to reproduce these effects in modern glass. His glistening and varied colors are of surpassing beauty and his forms original. Well known are the Tiffany *gold lustre*, an iridescent old gold, *Samian red, Mazarin blue,* which has a purplish shade, *Tel-el-amana*, or turquoise shading to peacock-green, and *Aqua Marine*, the color of deep water with bronze lights, or a paler green against which objects seem to float in water.

The forms of Tiffany glass owe nothing to the traditional Bohemian or Venetian influence. They are based rather on classical and Japanese prototypes. Since no piece was exactly duplicated, each one is a distinctive conception. The body of the glass, even when apparently frail, is strong and durable.

The peculiar decorations of Favrile glass are produced by the incorporation of different colors in the metal itself while it is in plastic condition, with subsequent manipulation. The contrasting layers are pulled and twisted by hooks to form a floral or other design. The example in Plate 27 illustrates the extraordinary skill displayed in this type of handling.

In spite of the splendid coloring and individual character of Tiffany glass, its almost metallic appearance belies the nature of the material. In this respect, it is not successful as glass.

Plate 27

TIFFANY "FAVRILE GLASS" VASE

*The decorative design, resplendent with iridescent peacock blue and green coloring,
is an integral part of the glass*

Plate 28

a) GILLINDER CRACKLE
GLASS BOWL

*Made by Gillinder Brothers,
Port Jervis, New York.
The fluted sides of this glass
are well suited for supporting
the stems of flowers*

b) BLOWN NASTURTIUM
VASE

*Simple flower holders of
clear or deep green glass
were made at the Union
Glass Company, Somerville,
Massachusetts, about 1900.
They are of various forms
well adapted to their use*

~~~~~~~~~~~~~~~~~~~~~~~~~~~~~~~~~~~~~

Chapter eight

Modern Glass

NO DATE CAN BE SET FOR THE TIME WHEN GLASS SHOULD BE CALLED "modern." One might apply the term to ware made since World War I, or one might go back to 1900, or even earlier. In describing machine-made products, the expression *modern* may even be a misnomer, since pressed glass, with enough change of pattern to bring it up to date, has reverted to the styles of the Victorian era. Cheaper ornamental glass, too, however made, smacks of Victorian taste. Only in the very finest and in the very cheapest glass do we find a change of mood.

In the early twentieth century, much of the best hand-made glass was imported from England, France, and Germany. Webb's English cameo, as well as the exquisite cameo carvings of Gallé and Daum, were received with appreciation in America, where nothing so ambitious was attempted. An enormous quantity of pressed and blown ware of more modest type was imported from Baccarat. This included tableware and toilet articles, colored, gilded, or painted, and blown-molded glass in pleasing and appropriate forms. Blown ware decorated with gilded engraved design was brought from Bohemia. These importations undoubtedly influenced the trend of American design.

The major output of the American flint-glass houses in the period around 1900 was cut ware. The older generation remembers only too well the tremendous quantities of such glass, good, bad, and mediocre, that flooded the market before World War I. At that time, glass was no longer valued for its fluid quality, but only for its sparkle and splendor as expressed in a superfluity of cutting.

As previously noted, this lavish use of prismatic cutting was introduced to the public at the time of the Centennial. In the decades immediately following, it rang all the possible changes for such work and thereafter began to degenerate. An 1880 catalogue shows that the cutting of that decade was entirely geometric and was carried out in large fields that almost covered the objects. The early "strawberry," or cross-hatched, diamond was revived and used with taste on excellent flint glass. A *hobnail diamond* and the *hob and star* design, which was copied in the cheapest pressed glass (the *daisy and button* pattern), and numerous variations of right-angle or diagonal cutting sufficed to produce dazzling effects. When the decoration was not of all-over character, bottoms of dishes and decanters were often star-cut.

Much of the 1880 cut glass can be admired today for its fine metal and careful workmanship. It cannot, however, be compared with eighteenth-century handcraft, for its mechanized perfection and measured contours rob it of the individual quality that graces early work.

Many of the forms illustrated in the Plates continued in use for thirty or more years. But there were some changes. Standing celery holders and spoon glasses were retired in favor of trays, castor sets disappeared, as did butter pats and gas globes, while tableware in general became heavier and thicker in order to allow for deeper cutting. By 1910, cut glass, a quantity product, had become the ideal of every middle-class bride. Except on more costly pieces, good design had given way to carelessly executed stars, pinwheels, and prismatic slices on mediocre metal shaped by pressing. There is nothing to be said for these wares.

Although cutting has been continued to the present day, it is now far more often inspired by the judicious craftsmanship of an earlier era than by its immediate antecedents. In the 1920's, rock crystal, or shallow slice, cutting replaced to a great extent the sharper prisms of the preceding decades. This style was expressed in patterns of garlands, leaves, arabesques, and conventional flowers. In the future it will probably be adjudged a weak type of design.

The early years of the century did, at least, bring some relief from the futilities of merely ornamental glass. The idea arose that vases and flower holders should be really functional. At least one glasshouse, the Union Glass Company of Somerville, Massachusetts, made a whole series of

Plate 29

STEUBEN "MARINER'S" DISH

*Designed at Steuben by Sidney Waugh. The remarkably beautiful engraving
is enhanced by the perfection of the metal*

Plate 30

STEUBEN "MERRY-GO-ROUND" BOWL

This handsome example of wheel engraving was also designed by Sidney Waugh as a present from Mr. and Mrs. Truman to H.R.H. Princess Elizabeth on the occasion of her marriage

receptacles especially devised to hold different blossoms and named them accordingly. Vases for nasturtiums, sweet peas, carnations, roses, lilacs, daisies, and numerous other flowers were blown of clear flint glass or in the muted green so much favored at the turn of the century (Plate 28b). These glasses were slightly varied in thickness by the use of rib-pattern molds and had wavy rims designed to support the flower stalks. As simple, useful, and inexpensive objects, they were admirable.

Another serviceable household adjunct of the early 1900's was the "console" set, consisting of a shallow flower bowl and a pair of candle-sticks. This arrangement was later developed in more elaborate table sets with a greater number of candle holders or with candelabra. They were blown in color, ornamented in various ways, or pressed in decorative forms.

The various phases of the modern movement have, as in other hand-crafts, been expressed in glass. The use of the material in heavy masses, demonstrated many years ago by French and other Continental artists, has come to be generally accepted and approved in America. Molding, etching, and sculptural cutting or hewing have been employed for the modification of form without injury to plastic effect. Much of this ex-trinsic ornamentation has been based upon abstract design. Angular contours, both for form and decoration, have frequently replaced curves. An example of this type of design in its simplest form is the familiar square ash tray indented at the corners.

During the past twenty-five years, our large glass companies have made an infinite variety of pressed glass. Rarely now do they employ the mechanical process, as did Deming Jarves, for the purpose of showy design, but they do constantly create new and interesting forms. The uses of glass are so many and its production by this method so comparatively cheap that it is now within the reach of every buyer. Luxury glass, on the other hand, because of the high wages paid to craftsmen and the dependence on artist designers, is more costly than ever. By improved scientific methods, the highest technical efficiency has been achieved: modern table glass is, indeed, a thing of perfection. Such fine metal and such consummate skill have gone into its making that no further improvement in this direction can be expected. Nevertheless, modern American glass has inevitably been influenced by the machine and by a public accustomed to mechanical exactness. It is therefore wanting in that infinite variety that we see in natural forms, but never in the products of machines. From even the finest expressions of our industrial age we sometimes must turn for satisfaction to the irregularities of an earlier day or to the primitive glass handcraft of our own time.

Several contemporary glasshouses devoted to pressing also have a considerable output of hand-decorated tableware. This has sometimes been of original character, or, at least, has shown a disposition to get away from traditional styles. In this attempt, glass made for twentieth-century purposes is more successful than is the general run of goblets, wines, and other continuing forms. Eighteenth-century proportions are rarely improved upon in this era. On the other hand, efforts to make something absolutely new in the fashioning of blown stem ware have not always resulted in creating stabilized styles, but only fashions subject to change from year to year.

Once in a while a glasshouse turns out such an original conception as the blown bowl in Plate 28a. This is an example of a recent revival of crackle glass by the Gillinder Brothers of Port Jervis, New York. Although this company is devoted to the manufacture of lighting equipment, it has nevertheless succeeded in devising some unusual and attractive flower holders. The bowl is of thick glass, hand ground on base and rim. Its fluted sides are especially well adapted to keep flowers in position, and its crackled surface reflects the light pleasantly.

Cut decoration of the past thirty years has often been really charming. Rock crystal cutting has continued in favor, becoming ever more and more abstract in design. Conventional floral compositions are not so often seen as are simple arrangements of lines, dots, and other geometric figures. However designed, this cut decoration is often subordinated to the form and does then in proper manner emphasize it.

Color was revived after 1920. Today it is possible to buy table glasses for almost any color scheme. Black and white in combination have been used effectively, and ruby, blue, amber, and amethyst have taken the place of the pale greens and pinks of thirty years ago. These gay colors are to be found in pressed glass as well as in the finer flint wares.

Handsome clear glass, however, will always be in demand. Today it is being supplied in reproductions of eighteenth-century forms and techniques. Notable achievements in this field have been made by the Blenko Glass Company, of Milton, West Virginia. At the present time this company is making faithful copies of the Colonial glasses unearthed at Williamsburg. The work is done entirely by hand, and the modern metal alone distinguishes some of the air-twist wines, blown decanters, or pitchers from their prototypes. It is also turning out many glasses of original style in more modern feeling. Some of these have simple, but effective, applied ornamentation, while others are self-decorated by large bubbles enclosed in the glass. A glass shot with fine air bubbles is also employed for blowing useful, but well-proportioned forms. Such colors as sea-green, sky-blue, turquoise, amethyst, ruby, emerald, and chartreuse give variety to Blenko's recent productions. This glass works is noteworthy for the high quality of its worksmanship and the functional design of its wares (Plate 32).   *169746*

Although it is here impossible to discuss in detail all the different companies that give us our modern glass, it will not be out of place to mention another that has made an outstanding contribution to the glassmaker's craft in America. This is the Steuben Glass Company of Corning, New York. Because this division of the great Corning Glass Works has been fostered by the parent concern, it has been enabled to pursue a course of artistic creation partly independent of sales considerations. With this objective in mind, Arthur Amory Houghton Jr., great-grandson of Corning's founder, reorganized the Steuben company in 1933, engaging his friends John Monteith Gates and Sidney Waugh, sculptor, as artistic advisers and directors. His first concern was to produce a flint glass that would surpass all others in clarity and brilliance. The efforts of a large corps of chemists succeeded so well in this endeavor that the peerless quality of Steuben metal is now generally acknowledged. Working together, the three enthusiasts then sought to originate forms and decorations along lines similar to the work of Swedish and Danish craftsmen. Up to this time, glass design had been left partly to the talents of master glassblowers, who had naturally relied upon traditional ideas. Henceforth, it was to be taken outside the blowing room. Whether glass conceived in the minds of artists who are not themselves glassmakers, but who have nevertheless tried to think in terms of glass techniques, is wholly successful must await the judgment of future generations.

The most noteworthy creations that have come out of this arrangement have been the plain blown vessels with sculpturesque figures for intaglio engraving designed by Sidney Waugh. Seen through the transparent crystal, these wheel carvings have the appearance of bas-reliefs. The aura of fancy that imbues the work places it in the category of fine art, and as such it is recognized. The two examples of Waugh's imagery shown in Plates 29 and 30 are particularly felicitous in that the engravings emphasize the forms of the objects in a highly desirable manner. This is not true of all Steuben vessels so decorated.

Another type of work executed by Steuben artisans is the cutting-away of thick vases with the intention of modifying their shape to stronger lines. A notable example of this style is the massive cut vase designed by Gates, which was exhibited at the Paris International Exposition of 1937. The judicious slicing away in contiguous flutes of the original blown wall of this piece has yielded a beautifully proportioned vessel that has brilliance along with solidity.

The insistence on hand manipulation and hand decoration has reaped its reward at Corning in the production of a great variety of tableware in original forms well suited to their uses and in simple engraved orna-mentation that follows the contours of the glasses. Vases, flower holders, and bowls are often perfectly plain, except for some slight enhancement by applied, tooled material (Plate 31). Recently this company has referred back to the traditional eighteenth-century shapes for drinking glasses. It is a round that must be followed again and again, with something new emerging in each generation. These forms are our heritage, the foundation of our glass culture. It is to be hoped that the newer creations of our own time may also prove of such worth that they, too, will one day be a valued part of our tradition.

Plate 31

STEUBEN "LOTUS" VASE

Blown at Steuben, this piece is given a feeling of strength by the hand-tooled applied gadroonings

Plate 32

BLENKO BLOWN PITCHER

Although a producer of fine clear flint glass, the Blenko Glass Company, of Milton, West Virginia, also makes bubble-flecked glass like this in a number of colors

Bibliography

Bergstrom, Evangeline H.: *Old Glass Paperweights*. The Lakeside Press, Chicago, Ill. 1940.

Chipman, Frank W.: *The Romance of Old Sandwich Glass*. Sandwich Publishing Co., Inc., Sandwich, Mass. 1932

Hunter, Frederick William: *Stiegel Glass*. Houghton Mifflin Co., Boston and New York. 1914.

Jarves, Deming: *Reminiscences of Glass-Making*. New York. 1865.

Knittle, Rhea Mansfield: *Early American Glass*. The Century Co., New York. 1927.

Lee, Ruth Webb: *Early American Pressed Glass*. Pittsford, N.Y. 1931.
    The Boston and Sandwich Glass Company. Framingham, Mass. 1938.

Lee, Ruth Webb, and James H. Rose: *American Glass Cup Plates*. Northborough, Mass. 1948.

McKearin, George S. and Helen: *American Glass*. Crown Publishers, New York. 1941.

Moore, N. Hudson: *Old Glass, European and American*. Frederick A. Stoles Company, New York. 1924.

Skelley, Leloise Davis: *Modern Fine Glass*. Richard R. Smith, New York. 1937.

Swan, Frank H.: *Portland Glass*. Providence, R.I. 1939 (2nd ed. 1949).

Van Rensselaer, Stephen: *Early American Bottles and Flasks*. Peterborough, N.H. 1928.

Watkins, Lura Woodside: *Cambridge Glass, 1818–1888*. Marshall Jones Co., Boston and Francestown, N.H. 1931.

Waugh, Sidney: *The Art of Glass Making*. Dodd, Mead, New York. 1937.

Weeks, Joseph D.: *Report on the Manufacture of Glass* (Census of 1880). Washington, 1884.

Much information can also be found in the files of *The American Collector* and *Antiques* ; the latter issued special Glass numbers, dated August 1933, July 1935, August 1937 and August 1941.

DATE DUE			
GAYLORD			PRINTED IN U.S.A